Positive Affirmatic
Power of Neuroscience and
Bioenergetics
Transform Your Life Through Information Fields

Frederico Honório

Catalographic data

ISBN	**9798858531951**
Number of pages	136
Edition	1 (2023)
Format	Book / E-Book
Finishing	Digital
Colouring	Black and white
Type of paper	*
Language	English

I want to dedicate this book to the driving forces of my constant learning, my wife Tainara, my children Nuno, Tatiana, Leónidas and Inaê and my mother, Eva, who always shows me the way

Prologue

Over the course of several years, whether as a therapist or later as a teacher of integrative therapies, I have observed the power that positive affirmation has in people's lives and how it impacts their entire system. This impact is not only in the alteration of the mental field of the individual, helping in his cognitive processes, but also in the emotional processes, expanding his range of resistance to everyday damage. Another observation that we can make, even from the reports that come to me from the active therapists trained by the CQM® Institute, is that on a spiritual level the impact is also very positive.

I want to make clear what I mean by spiritual. At the beginning of the 20th century, intellectual intelligence concerned the amount of information absorbed by the individual and his ability to respond, in quality and time to a given dilemma and had the name of Intellectual Quotient - IQ. This system has been widely used to evaluate human profiles in many areas of human knowledge. However, in the mid-90s of the last century, researchers in cognitive and behavioral science began to observe that intelligence was governed by processes and mechanisms far more complex than simple synaptic exchanges. So the genius was the one who knew how to deal with emotions, who had emotional intelligence – EQ because he knew how to apply the right emotion to each situation. His mental and emotional balance allowed him to act as expected for the success of the dilemma, even in the face of a situation of pressure or stress and to be able to apply the best qualities in the worst moments, without letting the emotion take the field of action. According *to Daniel Goleman*, author of the book *The Emotional Intelligence* [1,] this intelligence allows to study the context and choose the most appropriate emotion, choosing the most appropriate behavior within the limits of the situation and the individual freedom of the actors.

With the entry into the new millennium and new studies of human behaviors, especially beginning to notice more the movements called the *New Age* with the advent of the *internet* that aroused the interest of researchers in important areas such as sociology, psychology, theology and even neuroscience, there were discoveries that pointed to a third intelligence, the Spiritual Intelligence - QS that speaks of the action of the spirit.

This intelligence provides the choice of acts that have a greater meaning and that bring a benefit not only to the individual (who feels rewarded and happy) but to all of humanity.

But this Spiritual Intelligence is not to abdicate comfort, nor to take a vow of poverty or give alms, or to participate in a religious group, as the individual belief of each of us may anticipate. Spiritual Intelligence is the language of the Inner Self, of our Inner Master, it is the essence on which everything human fulfillment depends. Spiritual intelligence is the transforming power that can happen with simple actions in everyday life, in the family and at work, and in all the interrelations of the Being. It is also important to note that today, Spiritual Intelligence also has its application in the business world because it is a key to awaken mutual trust, improving the quality of negotiations between employers and employees, companies and unions and even between countries, and how much the individual gives himself to what he believes. In our view, the QS is the Purpose Quotient of the individual and is directly related to their healthy state.

When we think about the word and how its verbalization has an impact on our lives, it is impossible not to talk about the contribution of Neurolinguistic Programming to the healing of various behavioral, social and even business aspects today. Neuro-linguistic programming (NLP) is a designation that encompasses the three components increasingly influential in the production of human experience: neurology, language and programming. The neurological system regulates how our bodies work, language determines how we relate to and communicate with other people, and our programming determines the kinds of models of the world we create. Neurolinguistic Programming is a technique based on the dynamics between mind (neuro) and language (linguistics) and how their interaction affects our body and behavior (programming).

NLP is a multidimensional process, far beyond what is observable. which involves the development of behavioral competencies and flexibility, but also involves purpose-directed thinking and an understanding of the mental and cognitive processes behind behaviors and emotional processes. It provides tools and skills for the development of states of individual excellence, but it also establishes a system of empowering beliefs and presuppositions about what human beings are, what communication is, and what the process of change is. On another level, NLP is about self-discovery, exploring identity and mission. It also provides a framework for understanding and relating to the "spiritual" part of the human experience that goes beyond us as individuals to our family, community, and global systems. NLP is not only translated by *psychobioemotional* training that brings competence and excellence, but above all it is an adjunct tool of the individual that brings him wisdom (new knowledge or change of perspectives of the current reality) and vision (how he looks at his reality in a different way).

The other aspect to take into consideration is the way our change in the way we see the world, change our reality, changes the somatizing body, the physical body.

More advances in science, more discoveries that lead us to understand that the Healing we all desire and seek is actually an intimate process of renewal and transcendence. Picking up on a buzzword attributed to one of humanity's great Avatars, never has "*Your faith saved you*" made so much sense. With the research of the emeritus *Dr. Bruce Lipton*, transcribed in his works *The Biology of Belief*[2] *and* Spontaneous Evolution[3]*, we can understand* that a change in behavior, an exchange of harmful experiences for enriching experiences can make a process of self-healing and reverse complicated clinical pictures. Our faith, that is, what we believe in at the moment, which is the current reality, can save us, take us out of destructive processes whether on a physical, cognitive or emotional level and raise us to a level of transcendence, that is, of entry into our life purpose, into our spirituality. This is without using any kind of chemical remedy, dependence on third parties or needing to be an *expert* in these matters. Have you ever wondered how extraordinary we humans are?

The purpose of this book is not to burn stages in the personal development of each one, nor to be a definitive compendium for any therapist who wants to use the tools we bring, because I defend that we are always evolving and that to be integral, we have to study first and then apply. My goal is to bring together the knowledge of the Three Intelligences, NLP and the advances of Neuroscience in the field of Human DNA Regeneration and bring all this to the field of immediate application in an uncomplicated way.

May reading be fruitful and may contribute to the personal, human and professional development of the reader.

Frederico Honório

The Power of the Word

Speaking of spirituality, we have to bring it into our reality. We are in a world that is governed by Cartesian coordinates, that is, our greatest perception of the world revolves around length, width and height, that is, in three dimensions. Our perceptions are based on our physical sense organs, which always position us in this reality and with which we have always been accustomed to coexist. With the expansion of consciousness and the advent of some spiritualist doctrines that began to have expression around the 60s of the last century, a new wave of people began to appear and use a sixth sense, more focused on field reading in this Cartesian space, not so focused on what the physical senses brought, but for other sensations, emotions that were transmitted by capturing waves invisible to the naked eye, which they call spirituality and which we recognize as other dimensions.

Our reality, despite accessing other dimensions, is a three-dimensional reality and the physics of our world, the paradigm of consciousness that still hovers on our planet, forces us to verbalize what we bring within us so that they can understand us. The main communication process is then done by the voice or sign language, that is, our persona is revealed through the communication processes and this reveals our spirit.

With this we can affirm that the word of man is the Spirit in man. Words are sounds caused by the vibrations of thoughts, which in turn originate through the experience of the individual and are organized into pockets of information, divided between mental and emotional processes and are decoded by the processor we call the brain. This will define whether the thought, the action taken or the word spoken generate a normal flow movement, which does not go against any belief or standard instituted by the individual as his reality and thereby "order" the body to produce in a balanced way all the healthy chemistry, or, if it somehow contradicts its beliefs and standards and "messes" with its consciousness, The brain will go into protective mode and generate escape mechanisms and with that discharge the information into the body so that it is prepared at any time to flee. This is what happens, for example, in stress, depression and anxiety. Abnormal amounts of noradrenaline are discharged to compensate for the adrenaline generated by the feeling of constant danger, just as absurd amounts of cortisol are injected by the adrenal glands to try to regulate body balance. Continuously it is extremely harmful to our body. Every word, thought or action that comes out of your mouth, your mind or your physical posture generates a powerful field of information that will be translated by your brain and then passed on to your body, acting at the atomic level throughout it.

Words in most people are lifeless because they are automatically cast into the ether, without being impregnated with the strength of spirit, of will, of truth. Much talk, exaggeration or falsehood used in connection with words is as a way to simulate a reality that communicators know how to get out of reality and are, therefore, harmful to themselves.

That is why often, the meditations, prayers, or words of such people do not produce any desired definitive change in the order of things. They are empty.

Every word you utter must be sincere, that is, every word you utter must represent not only the Truth, but also part of your realized soul strength. Words without soul strength are husks without corn. Words accompanied with the high frequencies of emotions, which are the words felt and not just spoken, are like vibratory cyclones that, when directed, will surely collide and shatter the barriers of difficulties and create the desired change.

With this, avoid, in the same way, speaking unpleasant words, even if they are true, because they also impact on the environment in which you are and by reflex, on the people to whom they are addressed. Although much contested by conventional science, *Masaru Emoto[4], the* Japanese photographer who had the wonderful idea of photographing frozen water molecules after being exposed to bad and good words and thoughts and making a photographic exhibition with the results, massified the concept that it is actually true that the word produces a harmful or beneficial effect. Later, the Nobel Prize in Medicine *Luc Montagnier,* with his research, confirmed that water does indeed have memory and that it stores the information it captures from the environment, whether chemical or waveform, as frequency. Between Emoto and Montagnier, other researchers such as Allois Gruber, Leonid Izvekov and Konstantin Korotkov, to name just a few, prove the same, some of them continuing to bring very interesting proposals. This is also to leave the idea of the impact of the word on environments and others. Words should be chanted according to inner convictions. Repeated words or affirmations with understanding of your value and your performance in the personal field, with feeling and confidence in the result before it appears will certainly move the Cosmic Vibratory Force that facilitates healing, aligning your purpose and will help in your difficulty. Just appeal to this Force with infinite confidence, pushing away all doubt and the spirit of seeking the desired result. If you don't, your attention, which is the force of attraction in the goal, will be diverted and diverted from your objective brand.

The last ingredient of this healing formula is a look at the will to let go of the old to make way for the new and enter the new reality. And when I speak of this I always remember the famous phrase of Hippocrates in his speech that influences (or should influence) to this day the thought of the health professional: *"Before you heal someone, ask him if he is willing to give up the things that made him sick."*

The God-given Power to Man

It must be remembered that there is nothing greater in power than the Cosmic Consciousness or God, Allah, or Universe, or Great Architect, whatever you want to call or designate it. It exists. There is more than overwhelming evidence of his existence and of all that theology says about his presence, but that is a matter for another document. The Power of Cosmic Consciousness is greater than the power of your mind or the mind of others all as a whole, because in Truth, this Consciousness is the Great Set, the sum of all the pockets of information that sustain societies, planets, systems, galaxies and so on. We are part of the whole, we are little sparks of a God, who is a living organism and of which we are small self-existent and cooperating molecules. Thus, you should seek their help alone.

Remember that this Pulsating Force helps those who help themselves, because everything flows in cooperation and balanced exchange. We have in our possession, driven by the Creator, willpower, concentration, faith, reason and common sense to help you in your bodily or mental afflictions and which we have come to solidify with all the experiences accumulated along our path of transcendence. We must use all of them when seeking

divine help. Always during affirmations, prayer vibrations or in your meditation, feel that you are using your own divinity, but that it has to intertwine in coherence with the plural movement of all the other systems that surround you, to heal yourself or others. Always believe that it is not only this Divine Being, but also you who, as your extension of manifestation, tries to employ His will, reason, to react to the difficult problems of life, that is, let us remember another speech of popular wisdom: "*To God what is of God, to Caesar what is Caesar's.*"
The Divine Force is active throughout the Cosmos, but it is we who uniquely activate it. Without wanting to, there is no power.
During the different affirmations, the attitude of the mind must be different, for example, the affirmations of will must be accompanied by a strong will; to feel affirmations out of devotion; reason statements by intelligence and devotion; Affirmations of co-creation must be made already smelling the goal, because it begins there to materialize. When healing others, select that affirmation that is appropriate to your patient's conactive, co-creative, regenerative, emotional, or thoughtful temperament. In all affirmations, the intensity of attention comes first, but continuity and repetition also count for a lot, as they form a healing frequency block that breaks down all the blockages that make the individual unhealthy.
He imbues his statements with certainty of their effectiveness, because this is so, intensely and repeatedly, and the results will come naturally as the fruit of his work in favor of balance. During the process of physical healing,

attention should not be on the disease, but on the healing.

During mental healings of fear, anger, any bad habit, awareness of failure, failure, nervousness, intolerance concentration must be on the opposite mental quality, for example, the cure for fear is to cultivate the consciousness of bravery or love; from anger to peace; from weakness to strength and so on.

Mental Responsibility for Chronic States

When trying to get rid of a physical or mental illness through mental or physical methods, the person usually focuses more on the overwhelming power of the disease than on the possibility of cure, and thus allows the disease to be both a mental and physical habit. This is especially true in most cases where the disease is felt long after it has been physically cured. Each physical activity or bodily sensation of disease or health opens grooves in the brain cells, which automatically awaken certain habits of disease and causes the risk of a relapse, usually even more chronic, to be present; The subconscious habit of the disease or the awareness of health exerts a strong influence on the continuity of chronic diseases. Chronic mental or physical illnesses always have deep roots in the subconscious mind, or as we said in the CQM® Method, that which we cannot reference in the Concrete Mental Body and that comes from the Subjective and Emotional Mental Bodies, passes to the Physical Body as an anomaly and it becomes fertile ground for the installation of the disease. In a mental or physical disorder, one must be able to uproot its roots in the subconscious mind, that is, to signify what one does not understand. This is why all the claims practiced by the conscious mind must be impressive enough to remain as mental habits in the subconscious mind, which in turn would again automatically influence the conscious mind. The strong conscious affirmation being thus reinforced reacts in the mind and body through the subconscious.

Even stronger conscious will or convinced affirmations, based on the meaning of what is not understood, reach not only the subconscious, but also the superconscious, the magical deposit or factory of all the miraculous mental powers, which cause such miracles of medicine or radical changes in the individual, even on the family or financial plane, to take place.

Individual affirmations should be practiced willingly, with feeling, intelligence, and devotion, from time to time out loud (so that the resonance of the mantra sings more vigorously in all cells and all bodies), but mainly mentally (with the knowledge of the cause of the illness or blockage), with increasing intensity of attention and continuity. Attention from the beginning of the affirmation should constantly increase and should never be allowed to weaken.

Attentive and intelligent repetition and patience are the creators of habits, and as such should be employed in all affirmations. These deep and ongoing affirmations to heal chronic mental or bodily afflictions must be practiced mentally until they become almost an integral part of the person's intuitive routines, totally ignoring the unchanged or contrary results (if any), not to take the focus away from the healing, but not to get caught up in the tangle of questions it raises from the time it takes. In fact, knowing that the cure has already arrived, even without visible results, brings a component that is essential for the individual to relax and stop producing harmful substances. We talk about *placebo*, something that is often brought to the field when we talk about integrative therapies, especially energy therapies.

According to a 2016 Scientific *American[5] article* by award-winning journalist *Gareth Cook*, *"Placebo effect can be a confusing term as it has several different meanings. It is sometimes used to cover anyone who feels better after receiving placebo treatment (in the sense of false), which obviously includes all people who would have improved anyway. But researchers are finding that taking a placebo can also have specific, measurable effects on the brain and body."*

As neuroscientist *Fabrizio Benedetti*, one of the pioneers of placebo research, says, there is not just one placebo effect, but many. Placebo painkillers can trigger the release of natural pain-relieving chemicals called endorphins, which are neurohormones. Patients with Parkinson's disease respond to placebos with a flood of dopamine, a neurotransmitter. Fake oxygen, given to someone at altitude, has been shown to reduce levels of neurotransmitters called prostaglandins (which dilate blood vessels, among other things, and are responsible for many of the symptoms of altitude sickness). The fantastic thing about Placebo is that no substance enters the body, even to stimulate something. It is the focus on what one is possibly receiving that causes the brain to activate the areas of the body so that it naturally produces them.

None of these biological effects are caused by the placebos themselves, which are by definition inert. They are triggered by our neurological response to these "fake" treatments. The active ingredients are complex and not fully understood, but they include our expectation that we will feel better (which in turn is affected by all sorts of factors, such as our previous experience with the treatment, how impressive or invasive a treatment is, and whether we are optimistic about the outcome) and feeling heard and cared for.

Research to do in the future includes provoking the factors that shape placebo responses and investigating why conscious placebos (where someone knows they are taking a placebo) seem to work as well. Scientists also want to define exactly what conditions placebos work for (most research so far is on some model systems, such as pain, depression, and Parkinson's) and for whom they work (both genetics and personality seem to play a role).

And this was just one of many lines of research that tell us that the brain plays a big role in determining the level of pain we feel. Of course, any physical damage is important, but it is not enough or necessary for us to feel pain. So I think our approach to pain is totally wrong. Our focus is almost exclusively on trying to ban you with drugs, which are incredibly expensive and cause huge problems with side effects and addiction. Research like *Snow World* shows the potential of psychological approaches to pain management: both to maximize the effectiveness of drugs and, perhaps, in some cases, to replace them.

What Cure? The Vital Energy

Drugs, medicines, massages, spinal adjustment or treatment by healing frequencies help to bring back the harmonious condition lost of the cells by the amount of chemicals in the blood or stimulation of certain tissues. These are external methods that, although some are invasive, sometimes help the vital energy to effect a cure.

Without vital energy, all adjuvants cannot have any healing effect on the human body. Therefore, it can be seen that it is only the vital energy that can effect a cure; All external methods of stimulation can only cooperate with the vital energy and are powerless without it. And what is this vital energy (VE)?

To answer, let's start the other way around. Whenever our mental and emotional field is turned upside down, that our life seems like a pit of unsolved dilemmas, that we look at ourselves and don't like what we see, our body collapses. And we feel extreme tiredness, the desire to isolate ourselves from everything, including what can do us good. We can say that the vital energy is drained, because it is common to express that we do not have it for anything. This happens every time by sabotage and accommodation of the individual, because it never ends, but we run out of resources to stimulate and renew it. So vital energy is all that is in our environment to promote health movements. I don't want to talk about the cosmic, spiritual energies that are commonly talked about when we explore the concept of VE, because it's easier to assimilate than our pet, a well-spent afternoon with the family, a good book, a walk in the woods, do more VE capture than a meditation or a treatment. While treatment and meditation are around techniques and there is not always the understanding of how they work (which is extremely important for the individual to assimilate what they are receiving), the activities I mentioned earlier flow naturally without requiring knowledge or confidence to apply and bring a very great sense of satisfaction that they fill with gratitude.

"*The benefits associated with gratitude6 include better sleep, more exercise, reduced symptoms of physical pain, lower levels of inflammation, lower blood pressure, and a host of other things we associate with better health,*" said *Glenn Fox*, an expert in the science of gratitude. at the *University of Southern California.* "*The limits of the health benefits of gratitude are really in everything you pay attention to in feeling and practicing gratitude.*"

Scientific evidence from research on gratitude supports some typical approaches, including thanking people who don't expect it and writing down a few things every day that make you grateful.

"*It's very similar to working out, the more you practice, the better it gets,*" *Fox* said. *The more you practice, the easier it will be to feel gratitude when you need it.*"

Fox began researching gratitude as a doctoral student in neuroscience at *USC.* Some people scoffed at his interest in emotion, and it had received little attention from researchers. But he moved forward with what would become the first study of how gratitude manifests itself in the brain.

He found links between gratitude and brain structures also linked to social bonding, reward, and stress relief. Other studies have bolstered their findings, revealing connections between the tendency to feel grateful and a chemical called oxytocin, the well-known love molecule that promotes social bonds.

Research on gratitude has also found associations with other health benefits, including overall well-being, better sleep, more generosity and less depression. *Fox* said it makes sense that gratitude is beneficial from an evolutionary perspective. "*Gratitude is such an important function of our social lives and our evolution as a species,*" he said. *People who did not develop gratitude or grateful relationships with others, it is very unlikely that they would have survived in a social context.*"

Other USC experts also see building connections with others through gratitude as a critical part of prosperity in all plans.

Ilene Rosenstein, a psychologist and associate vice provost for wellness and education on the USC *campus*, encourages students and others to find a way to strengthen social bonds, even if they're not in the family home or haven't celebrated the holiday in the past. "*There's something wonderful about getting together with people and being grateful*," she said. *So you may not be able to be with your family or loved ones, but it can be a time to be brave and ask other people to come together – it doesn't have to be fancy."*

However, self-suggestion can be ineffective for acting on the type of man characterized by a strong belief that limits him. To speak of all this to a man who lives trapped in the mechanistic concepts of consumerist society can even cause the therapist to be seen as ridiculous. A deep analysis in the anamnesis to know how far one can go with so-and-so is as important in the therapeutic process as the application of the technique itself. He needs stimulation of his willpower, so that his convictions are dismantled and thus open the doors to be cured of his disease.

It is known, for those who research about "spontaneous miracles" the case of the dumb man who came out screaming from the burning house. The sudden shock produced by the sight of the fire so stimulated his feelings that he cried out, "Fire! Fire!" without remembering that until then he could not speak. A strong emotion overcomes the habit power of subconscious mental illness. This story illustrates the power of intense attention, which should be used in connection with affirmations to heal bodily ailments.

Will, focus, reason, or feeling, cannot by themselves effect a physical healing.

They act only as different agents that, according to the different behaviors of different individuals, can stimulate the vital energy to awaken and cure a certain disease. In a case of paralysis of the arm, if the will or focus is continuously stimulated, then the vital energy will suddenly rush to the diseased nerve channels, healing the tissues and the paralyzed arm. The repetition of affirmations must be firm and continuous so that they are sufficient to stimulate uncontrolled or inactive vital energy.

Two Factors in Healing

When planting a tree, two things should be considered: the proper seed and a good soil. So also in the cure of unhealthy states, two factors must be taken into account – the technique of the facilitator and the receptivity of the patient, who must respond to the therapist's requests.
The therapist's technique refers to his or her ability to apply the proper theories and methods to help the patient cope with their problems. This includes the ability to create a safe and welcoming therapeutic environment, to establish a relationship of trust with the patient, and to tailor the therapeutic approach according to the individual needs of each patient. A competent therapist must possess effective interpersonal skills, active listening ability, empathy, and specialized knowledge to treat different conditions and symptoms.

The receptivity of the patient is his ability to engage in the therapeutic process and to accept the support offered by the therapist. This includes commitment to the therapeutic process, openness to change, and involvement in activities and tasks aimed at improving mental health. The patient's willingness to express emotions and thoughts and to work on their problems is an important factor in the success of therapy.

Both of these factors are equally important for healing, as a highly skilled therapist cannot succeed if the patient is not open to receiving help. Similarly, a motivated patient may not get the expected benefits if the therapist does not possess the skills and techniques necessary to help him. Therefore, the proper combination between the therapist's technique and the patient's receptivity is critical for successful therapy.

Faith is more important than Time

Instant healing of corporeal, mental, emotional, and spiritual ailments can occur at any time. The accumulated darkness of eons is dissipated at once by bringing the light in. You never know when he'll be healed, so don't expect a cure by appointment. Trust in Universal Law (not religious, *neurobiocosmic*), not time, will determine when healing will take place. The results depend on the correct awakening of the vital energy and the mental and emotional state of the individual.

It takes time to awaken a weakened will, faith or imagination in a patient suffering from chronic disease because their brain cells are marked with awareness of the habits of the disease.

Brain cells are the control center of the human body and are involved in every activity we perform. Neuroscience has been studying brain cells for many years, and many recent studies show that these cells have a unique memory. According to neuroscience, brain cells are able to retain information about our habits and experiences, including information about diseases we may have faced in the past. This cellular memory is what allows us to deal with similar situations in the future.

Before we explore how brain cells are marked with awareness of disease habits, we need to understand how brain cells work. The human brain contains about 100 billion brain cells, known as neurons, that communicate through connections called synapses.

Neurons are responsible for all brain functions, from thinking and memory to movement and breathing. When a neuron is activated, it sends an electrical signal through its synapses to other neurons, creating a complex network of communication that is the basis of all brain functions.

In addition to neurons, the brain also contains glial cells, which help support and protect neurons. Glial cells play an important role in memory formation and the regulation of the brain's immune system.

Now that we have a basic understanding of brain cells, we can begin to explore how they are marked with awareness of disease habits. According to neuroscience, when our body faces a disease, our brain cells are activated and begin to record information about the disease. This information is then stored in our cellular memory and used to help us deal with similar diseases in the future.

For example, if a person has contracted a severe flu in the past, their brain cells recorded the information about the illness and created a "memory" of the illness. This cellular memory can affect how the body reacts, identifying the state as "disease," to any of the stimuli that brought you the unhealthy state and easily catch a cold with a cooler wind.

Habits are behaviors that become automatic after frequent repetitions, which can lead to changes in the structure and function of the brain. For example, if a person exercises regularly, it can lead to changes in brain structure that make them more efficient at coordinating movements and processing sensory information. Similarly, a sedentary behavior can lead to detrimental changes in the structure and function of the brain.

Now, recent studies suggest that brain cells can become "marked" with awareness of disease habits, which can negatively affect the health of the brain and body as a whole. This labeling occurs through epigenetic modifications, which are chemical changes in DNA that do not change the sequence of nucleotides, but can alter gene expression.

According to Brazilian neuroscientist *Suzana Herculano-Houzel*, these epigenetic modifications can occur in any cell in the body, including brain cells. This means that the habits a person develops throughout life can have profound and lasting effects on brain and body health, especially if those habits are harmful, such as smoking or eating an unhealthy diet.

However, the good news is that it is also possible to reverse these epigenetic modifications by changing habits. In a 2014 study published in the Journal of Alternative and Complementary Medicine7, researchers found that meditation and yoga can help reduce stress levels and consequently reverse stress-related epigenetic modifications.

One of the factors contributing to habit creation is the brain's ability to automate behaviors through the formation of specific neural pathways. These routes, or neural circuits, are created by the consistent repetition of a behavior and are established by connections between brain cells. These connections are reinforced each time the behavior is repeated, which makes it easier to execute in the future.

According to neuroscience, when a disease becomes chronic, it can influence the way these neural pathways are formed, which leads to the creation of disease-specific habits. For example, a patient with chronic pain may become accustomed to avoiding activities that aggravate the pain, which can lead to reduced mobility. Over time, this behavior can become an ingrained habit, making it difficult to resume mobility even after pain treatment.

The formation of disease-specific habits can also lead to a vicious cycle, where the behavior perpetuates the disease and the disease reinforces the behavior. This can be seen in cases of eating disorders, where patients may develop dysfunctional eating behaviors that perpetuate the disorder and make recovery difficult.

Another approach used to change disease-specific habits is physical rehabilitation. This approach is commonly used in patients with brain injuries that affect mobility or other bodily functions. Physical rehabilitation involves the repetition of specific movements to strengthen the neural pathways associated with that function. Over time, these neural pathways are strengthened and the patient can regain lost function.

In summary, neuroscience suggests that brain cells are marked with awareness of disease habits, which can lead to the formation of disease-specific habits. However, the neuroplasticity of the brain means that it is possible to change these habits through behavioral interventions and physical rehabilitation. With time and practice, the brain can create neural pathways and healthier habits, leading to an improvement in the patient's quality of life.

Curing a disease is a complex process and many factors can influence its effectiveness. Time can be one of those factors, but faith can also play an important role in the healing process.

The human mind is a powerful tool. It can influence our perception of the world around us and even affect the way our body works. Faith is one of the ways our mind can influence our body.

Studies show that faith can have positive effects on the healing process. For example, a 2015 study published in the *Journal of Behavioral Medicine* found that breast cancer patients who had a strong belief in God had less pain and fewer symptoms of anxiety and depression than those who did not.

Another study, published in the scientific journal *The Lancet*, found that patients who were told they would receive prayers from others had a lower rate of complications after surgery than those who were not told.

These studies suggest that faith can have a positive effect on curing a disease, but how exactly does that happen? The answer may lie in the mind-body connection.

The mind-body connection is the idea, duly proven, that our thoughts, feelings, and beliefs can affect our body. For example, when we are stressed, our body produces stress hormones, such as cortisol, which can negatively affect our health. Similarly, when we are happy and relaxed, our body produces hormones like endorphins, which can have positive effects on our health.

Faith can help foster a positive mind-body connection. When we believe that we are being cared for by a greater power, we can feel a sense of peace and security. This can reduce stress and anxiety levels, which in turn can have a positive effect on our health.

In addition to the direct benefits of faith in curing an illness, faith can also offer important social support. Religious communities can offer emotional and practical support to their members, which can be especially important for those who are experiencing a health problem.

For example, research published in the *Journal of Health and Social Behavior* found that individuals who regularly attend religious services are more likely to have a wider social network and to receive emotional and practical support from their fellow believers.

Based on all the studies and examples we have presented, we can conclude that faith can be a powerful tool in healing diseases. While time is an important factor in the healing process, believing that it is possible to recover and have a positive attitude toward the disease can help speed up the process.

It is important to remember that faith is no substitute for medical treatments and should not be seen as a miracle cure for all diseases. However, believing in something bigger than ourselves can bring comfort and hope during difficult times.

Each individual has their own healing journey and what works for one may not work for another. Therefore, it is important to respect the beliefs and choices of each person in relation to their health.

Positive Affirmations and the Power of Neuroscience and Bioenergetics

Healing Classification

1. Healing of bodily ailments.
2. Healing from emotional illnesses that project feelings like fear, anger, bad habits, awareness of failure, lack of initiative, and confidence.
3. Cure of mental illnesses for lack of references, knowledge, meaning of dilemmas of your life or even various beliefs.
4. Healing of spiritual ailments such as ignorance, indifference, purposeless life, intellectual pride and dogmatism and theoretical metaphysics, skepticism and contentment with the mechanistic and material method of existence, ignorance of the laws of life and of one's own divinity.

It is of paramount importance that equal emphasis be given to the prevention and cure of all these four "types of disease" that we commonly call anomaly, since the normal state is Integral Health and the exit from normal is anomaly.

The attention of most people is focused only on the cure of bodily diseases, because these are tangible and obvious and do not require, apparently, major exercises of diagnosis, prognosis and healing procedure. They are almost standard, which in our view is a tremendous mistake, because with what we have already seen, we can easily realize that the therapeutic process is individual and that there may be cases with the same characteristics, but the different realities, based on the individual experiences of individuals makes their healing process also individual. Ignorance of the laws of mental and emotional hygiene and the spiritual art of living are responsible for all human bodily and material suffering. If the mind is free from the mental bacteria of anger, worry, fear, and the Soul is free from ignorance, no disease or material want will manifest in the field of the third dimension. We don't want diseases in the body, mind, or soul. We don't need medicine, nor mental or spiritual healing if we're okay. Out of ignorance we break the laws of harmony by which the body governs itself in third-dimensional experience, and then seek methods of healing. We want to be free from disease in every way and so all our concentration must be focused on the prevention of physical, mental and spiritual diseases.

Brain, that Quantum Computer

While talking to a student, we noticed that we both felt incredibly excited and anxious about the work we were doing at the moment, linked to the operation of the pendulum in capturing subtle energies, but we commented that this feeling was not easy to describe: it seemed that there was a bit of stress for the possible innovation that had resulted from the conversation, but not in a negative way.

This stress (with the same symptoms as harmful stress) was due to the result of some of our projects, but we also felt motivated and energized.

Worry, stress and anxiety are very common when putting in commitment and dedication, whether people love their job or not.

I recently did a metaphysical analysis of the concept of worrying and the stress and anxiety caused in movement and hypothesized if there was a sweet spot, something strong enough to motivate us to do our best to achieve our goals, but not strong enough to paralyze us? That is, do processes that are apparently harmful, such as stress and anxiety, have any point at which they become useful?

When I talk about stress or anxiety, I always remember to compare the picture with a high competition athlete.

When the body is stressed, the muscles become tense. Muscle tension is almost a reflex reaction to stress – the body's way of protecting itself against injury and pain, but also of being ready for escape, because the state of stress is signified by our reference system as a time of imminent danger.

With sudden-onset stress, the muscles tense all at once and then release their tension when the stress passes. Chronic stress causes the muscles of the body to be in a more or less constant state of caution. This is what happens to an athlete prepared to give everything during the test that will provide.

Musculoskeletal pain in the lower back and upper extremities has also been linked to stress, especially stress at work, which is also something that happens to athletes after high-competition exercise, so they have a whole recovery plan. Relaxation techniques and other stress-relieving activities and therapies have been shown to effectively reduce muscle tension, decrease the incidence of certain stress-related disorders such as headache, and increase feelings of well-being. For those who develop chronic pain conditions, stress-relieving activities have been shown to improve mood and daily function.

The respiratory system delivers oxygen to the cells and removes carbon dioxide waste from the body. Air enters through the nose and passes through the larynx into the throat, down the windpipe and into the lungs through the bronchi. The bronchioles then transfer oxygen to the red blood cells for circulation. Stress and strong emotions can present respiratory symptoms, such as shortness of breath and rapid breathing, because the airways between the nose and lungs contract, precipitating a smaller flow and therefore, in automatic reflex, there is a response of the body to maintain the amount through greater work of the system. For people without respiratory disease, this is usually not a problem as the body can manage the additional work to breathe comfortably, but psychological stressors can exacerbate breathing problems for people with pre-existing respiratory illnesses such as asthma and chronic obstructive pulmonary disease, something that is also common after exercise on the edge when you don't have a recovery plan.

Some studies show that acute stress — such as the death of a loved one — can trigger asthma attacks or anticipate a lung problem that has not yet revealed itself. In addition, rapid breathing — or hyperventilation — caused by stress can trigger a panic attack in someone prone to panic attacks.

Also here therapy to develop relaxation, good breathing and other cognitive-behavioral strategies can help.

The heart and blood vessels comprise the two elements of the cardiovascular system that work together in providing nutrition and oxygen to the body's organs. The activity of these two is also coordinated in the body's response to stress. Acute stress – momentary or short-term stress, such as meeting deadlines, getting stuck in traffic or suddenly hitting the brakes to avoid an accident – causes an increase in heart rate and stronger contractions of the heart muscle, with the stress hormones – adrenaline, noradrenaline and cortisol, acting as messengers of these effects, which, once again, is common in high competition athletes as proven by numerous studies.

When someone is in a challenging, threatening, or uncontrollable situation, the brain initiates a cascade of events involving the hypothalamic-pituitary-adrenal (HPA) axis, which is the primary driver of the endocrine response to stress and is what happens when an athlete prepares for their competition event.

During times of stress, the hypothalamus, a collection of nuclei that connects the brain and endocrine system, signals the pituitary gland to produce a hormone, which in turn signals to the adrenal glands, located above the kidneys, to increase cortisol production. Cortisol increases the level of available energy fuel by mobilizing glucose and fatty acids from the liver. Cortisol is normally produced at varying levels throughout the day, usually increasing in concentration upon waking up and slowly decreasing throughout the day, providing a daily cycle of energy and in balanced doses is extremely helpful, but in situations such as continued stress or preparation for competition, its production is exacerbated.

The gut has hundreds of millions of neurons that can function quite independently and are in constant communication with the brain which explains, for example, the ability to sense "butterflies" in the stomach, which is a phenomenon that occurs in both good and worse times. In the case under analysis, both stress and the competition event can produce it. Stress can affect this brain-gut communication and can trigger pain, bloating, and other intestinal discomforts that will be felt more easily. The gut is also inhabited by millions of bacteria that can influence your health and brain health, which can affect the ability to think and affect emotions. Stress is associated with changes in gut bacteria that, in turn, can influence mood. Thus, nerves and gut bacteria strongly influence the brain and vice versa.

Can you see where this situation often happens? That's right! Both in stress and in high competition athletes. It is important to bring this image, not only to realize that the individual produces the same metabolic effort as the high competition athlete, as the high competition athlete is constantly under stress. The difference is that the athlete is accompanied by coaches and techniques that produce a state of balance and prepare him for a test in a few days and the ordinary individual is rarely accompanied by a professional who can restore this balance.

After this parenthesis of contextualization, let's return to our hypothesis; Do processes that are seemingly harmful, such as stress and anxiety, have any point at which they become useful? Our conclusion is that seems to be the case...

In the children's story *The Three Bears*, attributed to English writer *Robert Southey*, Goldilocks tastes three different bowls of porridge and discovers that he likes porridge that is neither too hot nor too cold – but only at the right temperature. This concept is known as the Goldilocks Principle and has been used in various disciplines to describe something that is neither too high, nor too low – but just right, the balanced.

A recent research study in the British Journal of Psychiatry found that school-age children with high levels of anxiety performed poorly, but that children with very low levels of anxiety also did not perform well. This is the Goldilocks effect at play: we need an ideal level of anxiety so that we can give our best, a level of anxiety and stress that is optimal, so that the levels of focus and attention are present in the here and now. But lest you think that I am here saying that anxiety and stress, even in "balance" and right doses are good, which are not, we have to understand how our brain works.

One theory that is floated in the field of neuroscience is that anxiety levels are somehow correlated with how much you care about a specific task or a specific outcome. No anxiety means a total lack of interest and therefore poor performance results. Too much anxiety, on the other hand, has negative effects on performance, affecting your self-esteem and self-confidence. Some reasonable level of anxiety shows that an individual cares enough about the task at hand, but is still able to keep a clear mind. It's also why many people report performing better under pressure. You procrastinate for two weeks and then when the deadline is near, you work hard to get the job done and most of the time you don't produce good enough work, other times the result is fantastic.

What about stress? As is often the case with mental health, it's also a matter of balance. While anxiety originates from internal mechanisms of thought, reference and meaning that are linked to cognitive processes, stress is a response to external factors and has an emotional basis. Thousands of years ago, such external factors included the need to flee from a predator or other situations in which we needed to think and act as quickly as possible to ensure our survival.

That's why stress isn't inherently bad: When you're under stress and need to react quickly and stay alert, your brain releases cortisol, as we've already seen. This will increase your heart rate and blood pressure and divert resources from other tasks — such as inflammatory responses — to help your body focus on more immediate needs.

Cortisol also increases the plasticity of your brain: it means you're able to think and remember better. So short-term stress isn't bad for us, and our brain is actually designed to optimize our responses under stress: of the results analyzed in relaxed or pleasurable routine situations, about 10% of our cortisol receptors are normally busy, while the other 90% are just a reserve waiting for a stress response.

Stress becomes dangerous when it goes beyond those short bursts that are treated quickly. Cortisol is neurotoxic in large amounts and chronic stress is harmful. Parts of your neurons will shrink, some neurotransmitters that are good in small amounts but bad in large ones will be overproduced, and many other bad things will happen in your brain, often leading to mental illness. A little cortisol is good, a lot is bad. That's why cortisol is often called the "*stress currency*," and there's a lot of research going on right now targeting cortisol specifically to try to prevent or treat mental health problems.

And you might be wondering, "What does this have to do with the power of the word?" It has everything. When we do a mental or emotional reprogramming we must take into account these factors, because many of them are as easily distorted as they are misunderstood. Once upon a time, a fellow therapist said that she did not understand what was happening to a particular patient. She had executed the entire therapeutic process just right, but the result had been catastrophic. She reported that the patient no longer had the initial symptoms that led her to the appointment, but that she had developed an intestinal problem with some severity and a significant increase in cholesterol. The words "gut" and "cholesterol" soon made me ring the bell of metaphysical health references and this led me to some gut bacteria that are highly beneficial to us, known as probiotics. They are essential for the proper functioning of the intestine, as well as very important for the reduction of cholesterol levels. Speaking of this, she easily realized what had happened. During the reprogramming, she and the patient had executed a command to eliminate "all the bacteria in the body," when she should have specifically named those that were to eliminate or command the elimination of the bacteria harmful to the organism. The patient would have reproduced the command for approximately two weeks and the brain began the process of elimination, activating the internal means to do so. Fortunately, the colleague, after identifying the error, was able to successfully revert it.

But this is our brain. He commands. He drives. And he is irreverent and disobedient about the rules we think are the ones that "govern" us. Each brain produces its own reality, and this reality depends on the experience, belief, pattern of behavior and command of its operator.

Now, the Power of the Word

We are almost to the most desired moment and for which this book may eventually have caught your attention. But before we move on to the practical commands, let's finish the more "theoretical" part talking about neuroplasticity, which is essential for the regenerative healing process to take place. Neuro is the term that derives from "neuron," the nerve cells in our brains and nervous systems. Plastic means "changeable, malleable, modifiable."

At first, many of the researchers did not dare to use the word "neuroplasticity" in their publications, because, in fact, their colleagues belittled them for promoting a "fanciful" notion, far from the almost mechanical view of brain functioning. However, they persisted, slowly overthrowing the doctrine of the immutable brain. They showed that children are not always stuck with the mental abilities they were born with; that the damaged brain can often reorganize itself so that when one part fails, another can replace; that if brain cells die, they can sometimes be replaced; that many "circuits" and even basic reflexes that we think are rigidly programmed are not.

One of these scientists even showed that thinking, learning and acting can activate or deactivate our genes, our chemical and electrical structure, thus shaping our brain anatomy and our behavior, this was certainly one of the most extraordinary discoveries of the twentieth century and which perhaps we will talk about at length in an upcoming book. In the course of my investigations, I met technicians who using the right mental and emotional reprogramming allowed people blind from birth to begin to see, others who allowed deaf people to hear. This is not fiction, it is documented and duly proven; I've talked to people who had a cardiovascular accident decades before and were declared incurable with regard to sequelae and who had their recovery helped with neuroplastic treatments; I've met people whose learning disorders have been cured and whose IQs have increased; I've seen evidence, right next to me, that it's possible for eighty-year-olds to work on their memories and cognitive processes to function the same way they did when they were fifty-five. I've seen people rewiring their brains with their thoughts, to heal obsessions, schisms, behavior patterns, and traumas once considered incurable. In none of them have I been faced with "a miracle" or performed any.

The idea that the brain can change its own structure and function through thought and activity is, I believe, the most important change in our view of the brain since we sketched out its basic anatomy and the functioning of its basic component, the neuron. In fact, there is a whole architecture in this phenomenal machine that means all functions, from physical, mental, emotional or spiritual.

The neuroplasticity revolution has implications for, among other things, our understanding of how love, sex, grief, relationships, learning, addictions, culture, technology, and therapies change our brains. All the humanities, social sciences, and physical sciences, insofar as they deal with human nature, are affected, as are all forms of training. All of these disciplines will have to accept the fact that the brain changes automatically and the perception that the architecture of the brain differs from one person to another and that it changes in the course of our individual lives.

Neuroplasticity has the power to produce more flexible behaviors, as the name implies, but also more rigid, which seems contradictory. Ironically, some of our most stubborn habits and disorders are products of our plasticity. Once a certain plastic change occurs in the brain and becomes well established and referenced as truth, it can prevent other changes from occurring. It is by understanding the positive and negative effects of plasticity that we can truly understand the extent of human possibilities.

Michael Merzenich is a personality known to be a driving force behind dozens of neuroplasticity innovations and practical inventions. His name is the one most often praised by other professionals and investigators.

Irish neuroscientist *Ian Robertson* described him as "*the world's leading researcher in brain plasticity.*" *Merzenich's* specialty is improving people's ability to think and perceive by redesigning the brain and training specific processing areas, called brain maps, to do more mental and emotional work. He also, perhaps more than any other scientist, showed in rich scientific detail how our brain processing areas change.

Of the neuroplasticity professionals with solid scientific credentials, it was *Merzenich* who made the most ambitious claims for the field: that brain exercises can be as useful as medicines to treat diseases as serious as schizophrenia; that plasticity exists from cradle to grave; and that radical improvements in cognitive functioning— how we learn, think, perceive, and remember—are possible even in the elderly. His latest patents are for techniques that promise to allow adults to learn language skills without effort to memorize.

Merzenich argues that practicing a new skill, under the right conditions, can change hundreds of millions and possibly billions of connections between nerve cells in our brain maps.

If you who accompany us on this trip are skeptical of such spectacular claims, keep in mind that they come from a man who has already helped cure some disorders that were once considered intractable and all of them are properly documented. Early in his career, *Merzenich* developed, along with his group, the most commonly used design for the cochlear implant, which allows children with congenital deafness to hear.

Her current plasticity work helps students with learning disabilities improve their cognition and perception. These techniques – his series of plasticity-based computer programs, Fast *ForWord* (English linguistic play on the expression *Fast Forward* that loosely translated as Fast Effect Word or Fast Learning) – have already helped hundreds of thousands. *Fast ForWord* is disguised as a children's game. What's amazing about this is how quickly change occurs. In some cases, people who have had a lifetime of cognitive difficulties improve after only thirty to sixty hours of treatment.

Unexpectedly, or perhaps not, the program has also helped several autistic children. *Merzenich* states that when learning occurs in a manner consistent with the laws governing brain plasticity, the brain's mental "machinery" can be enhanced so that we learn and perceive with greater precision, speed, and retention.

Clearly, when we learn, we increase what we know. But *Merzenich's* claim is that we can also change the very structure of the brain and increase its ability to learn. Unlike a computer, the brain is constantly adapting.

"*The cerebral cortex,*" he says of the brain's thin outer layer, "*is actually selectively refining its processing capabilities to suit each task at hand.*"

The brain *Merzenich* describes is not a vassila we fill; rather, it is more like a living creature with an appetite, which can grow and change with proper nutrition and exercise. Prior to *Merzenich's* work, the brain was viewed as a machine with precision within the cognitive and emotional limits of the individual, but with unalterable limits of memory, processing speed, and intelligence. *Merzenich* showed that each of these assumptions is wrong.

He didn't come to understand how the brain changes, but he did come across the realization that the brain can rearrange its maps. And while he wasn't the first scientist to demonstrate neuroplasticity, it was through experiments he conducted early in his career that leading neuroscientists began to look at the plasticity of the brain from a new perspective, much closer to the models we have today.

To understand how brain maps can be altered, we first need to have a picture of them. They were first demonstrated in humans by neurosurgeon *Dr. Wilder Penfield* at the *Montreal Neurological Institute* in the 1930s.

For Penfield, "mapping" a patient's brain had to figure out, through observation, where in the brain different parts of the body were represented and their activities processed — a solid blueprint for localization. The "localizationists" discovered that the frontal lobes were the headquarters of the brain's motor system, which initiates and coordinates the movement of our muscles. The three lobes behind the frontal lobe, the temporal, parietal, and occipital lobes, comprise the brain's sensory system, processing the signals sent to the brain by our five sensory receptors— eyes, ears, touch, taste, and smell receptors.

Penfield spent years mapping the sensory and motor parts of the brain while performing brain surgeries on cancer and epilepsy patients who might be conscious during the operation because there are no pain receptors in the brain. Both sensory and motor maps are part of the cerebral cortex, which sits on the surface of the brain and is therefore easily accessible with a probe. *Penfield* found that when he touched the sensory map of a patient's brain with an electrical probe, it triggered sensations that the patient felt in his or her body. He used the electric probe to help him distinguish the healthy tissue he wanted to preserve from the unhealthy tumors or pathological tissue he needed to remove.

Normally, when the hand is touched, an electrical signal passes to the spinal cord and ascends to the brain, where it activates the map cells that make the hand appear touched. *Penfield* found that he could also make the patient feel that his hand was touched by electrically activating the hand area of the brain map. By stimulating another part of the map, the patient could feel his arm being touched, another part, his face. Each time he stimulated an area, he would ask patients what they felt, to make sure he hadn't cut healthy tissue. After many of these operations, he was able to show where, on the sensory map of the brain, all parts of the body's surface were represented.

He did the same with the motor map, the part of the brain that controls movement.

By touching different parts of this map, he could trigger movements in the patient's leg, arm, face, and other muscles.

One of Penfield*'s great discoveries* was that sensory and motor brain maps, like geographic maps, are topographic, meaning that areas adjacent to each other on the surface of the body are usually adjacent to each other in brain maps. He also found that when he touched certain parts of the brain, he triggered long-lost childhood memories or scenes of dreams already forgotten or seemingly forgotten — implying that higher mental activities were also mapped in the brain.

Penfield*'s maps* have shaped the view of the brain for several generations. But because scientists believed that the brain couldn't change, they assumed and taught that maps were fixed, immutable, and universal—the same in each of us—though *Penfield* himself, apparently, never made any of these claims.

Merzenich found that these maps are neither immutable within a single brain nor universal but vary in their boundaries and size from person to person. In a series of brilliant experiments, he showed that the shape of our brain maps changes depending on what we do throughout our lives. But to prove that point, he needed a much more precise tool than *Penfield's* electrodes, capable of detecting changes in only a few neurons at a time.

While studying at the University of *Portland, Merzenich* and a friend used electronic laboratory equipment to demonstrate the storm of electrical activity in the insects' neurons. These experiments caught the attention of a professor who admired *Merzenich's talent and curiosity and* recommended him for graduate studies at *Harvard* and *Johns Hopkins*. They both accepted it. *Merzenich* opted for *Hopkins* to do his Ph.D. in physiology with one of the great neuroscientists of the time, *Vernon Mountcastle*, who in the 1950s demonstrated that the subtleties of brain architecture could be discovered by studying the electrical activity of neurons using a new technique: micromapping with pin-shaped microelectrodes. Microelectrodes are so small and sensitive that they can be inserted into or next to a single neuron and can detect when an individual neuron fires its electrical signal to other neurons. The signal from the neuron passes from the microelectrode to an amplifier and then to the oscilloscope screen, where it appears as a sharp peak. *Merzenich* would make most of his major discoveries with microelectrodes.

This important invention allowed neuroscientists to decode the communication of neurons, of which the adult human brain has approximately 100 billion. Using large electrodes like *Penfield* did, the scientists were able to observe thousands of neurons firing at the same time. With microelectrodes, scientists could "listen" to one or several neurons at a time as they communicate with each other. The micromapping is still about a thousand times more accurate than the current generation of brain scans, which detect bursts of activity that last a second in thousands of neurons. But the electrical signal from a neuron usually lasts a millisecond, so brain scans lose an extraordinary amount of information. However, micromapping has not replaced brain scans because it requires an extremely tedious type of surgery, conducted under a microscope with microsurgical instruments.

Merzenich adopted this technology immediately. To map the area of the brain that processes hand sensation, *Merzenich* would cut a piece of a monkey's skull over the sensory cortex, exposing a 1- to 2-millimeter strip of the brain, and then insert a microelectrode next to a sensory neuron. Then he would tap the monkey's hand until it touched a part – such as, for example, the tip of a finger, which caused that neuron to fire an electrical signal on the microelectrode. It recorded the location of the neuron that represented the fingertip, establishing the first point on the map. Then he would remove the microelectrode, reinsert it near another neuron, and tap into different parts of the hand, until he located the part that connected that neuron. He did this until he mapped out the whole hand. A single mapping can require five hundred insertions and take several days or weeks, *and Merzenich* and his colleagues have done thousands of these laborious surgeries to make their findings.

Around this time, a crucial discovery was made that would forever affect *Merzenich*'s work. In the 1960s, when *Merzenich* was beginning to use microelectrodes in the brain, two other scientists, who had also worked at *Johns Hopkins* with *Mountcastle*, discovered that the brains of very young animals have plasticity, just like that of humans. *David Hubel* and *Torsten Wiesel* were micromapping the visual cortex to learn how vision is processed. They inserted microelectrodes into the visual cortex of kittens and found that different parts of the cortex processed the lines, orientations, and movements of visually perceived objects. They also found that there was a "critical period," from the third to the eighth week of life, when the newborn kitten's brain needed to receive visual stimulation to develop normally. In the crucial experiment, *Hubel* and *Wiesel* covered one eye of a kitten during its critical period so that the eye received no visual stimulation.

When they opened the closed eye, they found that the visual areas in the brain map that normally processed the entrance of the closed eye had not developed, leaving the kitten blind from that eye for the rest of its life. Clearly, the brains of kittens during the critical period were plastic, their structure literally shaped by experience, and this is very interesting for us to understand how mental reprogramming exercises and creates new areas of innovation and personal development in all areas.

When *Hubel* and *Wiesel* examined the brain map of that blind eye, they made yet another unexpected discovery about plasticity. The part of the kitten's brain that was deprived of information from the closed eye did not remain idle. It began to process visual information from the open eye, as if the brain did not want to waste any "cortical state" and had found a way to reconnect, which brings us another indication of the plasticity of the brain is in critical or crisis periods. For this work, *Hubel* and *Wiesel* received the Nobel Prize. However, although they discovered plasticity in childhood, they remained *localizationists*, espousing the idea that the adult brain is programmed in late childhood to perform functions at fixed locations.

The discovery of the critical period became one of the most famous in biology in the second half of the twentieth century. scientists soon showed that other brain systems needed environmental stimuli to develop. It also seemed that each neural system had a different critical period, or window of time, during which it was especially moldable and sensitive to the environment, and during which it had rapid formative growth. Language development, for example, has a critical period that begins in childhood and ends between the age of eight and puberty. After this critical period ends, a person's ability to learn a second language without an accent is limited. In fact, second languages learned after the critical period are not processed in the same part of the brain as the native language.

The notion of critical periods also supported ethologist *Konrad Lorenz*'s observation that newly born geese, if exposed to a human being for a brief period between fifteen hours and three days after birth, were attached to that person rather than to the mother. To prove it, he got the geese to bond with him and follow him. He called this process "*imprinting*." In fact, the psychological version of the critical period goes back *to Freud*, who argued that we go through developmental stages that are brief windows of time, during which we must have certain experiences to be healthy; these periods are formative, he said, and shape us for the rest of our lives.

The plasticity of the critical period changed medical practice. Because of *Hubel* and *Wiesel's* discovery, children born with cataracts no longer faced blindness. They were sent for corrective surgery as infants, during their critical period, so that their brains could get the light needed to form crucial connections.

Merzenich *'s first glimpse of* adult plasticity was accidental. In 1968, after completing his doctorate, he did postdoctoral work with *Clinton Woolsey*, a researcher in *Madison,* Wisconsin, and a colleague of *Penfield's*. *Woolsey* asked *Merzenich* to supervise two neurosurgeons, Drs. *Ron Paul* and *Herbert Goodman*.

The three decided to observe what happens in the brain when one of the peripheral nerves in the hand is severed and begins to regenerate. It is important to understand that the nervous system is divided into two parts. The first part is the central nervous system (brain and spinal cord), which is the command-and-control center of the system and which was thought to lack plasticity.

The second part is the peripheral nervous system, which carries messages from the sense receptors to the spinal cord and brain and carries messages from the brain and spinal cord to the muscles and glands. The peripheral nervous system has long been known to have plasticity, since, for example, if you cut a nerve in your hand, it can "regenerate" or heal itself.

Each neuron has three parts. Dendrites are tree-like branches that receive information from other neurons. These dendrites lead to the cell body, which sustains the life of the cell and contains its DNA. Finally, the axon is a living cable of various lengths (from microscopic lengths in the brain, to some that can descend to the legs and reach up to six feet in length). Axons are often compared to wires because they carry electrical impulses at very high speeds (from 3 to more than 300 kilometers per hour) toward the dendrites of neighboring neurons.

A neuron can receive two types of signals: those that excite it and those that inhibit it. If a neuron receives enough excitatory signals from other neurons, it will fire its own signal. When it receives enough inhibitory signals, it becomes less likely to fire. The axons do not touch neighboring dendrites. They are separated by a microscopic space called a synapse. Once an electrical signal reaches the end of the axon, it triggers the release of a chemical messenger, called a neurotransmitter, at the synapse. The chemical messenger floats up to the dendrite of the adjacent neuron, exciting or inhibiting it.

When we say that neurons "rewire," we mean that changes occur in the synapse, strengthening and increasing, or weakening and decreasing, the number of connections between neurons.

Merzenich, Paul *and Goodman* wanted to investigate the already known,   but as yet unexplained, interaction between the peripheral and central nervous systems. When a large peripheral nerve (consisting of many axons) is cut, sometimes in the process of regeneration, the "wires intersect." When the axons reattach to the axons of the wrong nerve, the person may experience a "false location," so that a tap on the index finger is felt on the thumb. The scientists assumed that this false location occurred because the regeneration process "shuffled" the nerves, sending the signal from the index finger to the thumb brain map.

The model the scientists had of the brain and nervous system was that each point on the surface of the body had a nerve that transmitted signals directly to a specific point on the brain map, anatomically connected at birth. Thus, a nerve branch to the thumb always transmitted its signals directly to the point on the sensory map from the brain to the thumb.

Merzenich and the group accepted this "peer-to-peer" model of the brain map and began to innocently document what was happening in the brain during this shuffling of nerves. They micromapped the hand maps into the brains of several adolescent monkeys, cut a peripheral nerve from the hand, and immediately stitched the two severed ends together but without touching, hoping that the nerve's many axon wires would intersect as the nerve regenerated. per se. After seven months, they remapped the brain. *Merzenich* assumed that they would see a very disturbed and chaotic brain map. Thus, if the nerves of the thumb and forefinger were crossed, he expected that touching the index finger would generate activity in the map area for the thumb. But he didn't see any of that. The map was almost normal. "*What we saw,*" *Merzenich says,* "*was absolutely astounding. I couldn't understand it.*" It was arranged topographically as if the brain had unscrambled the signals from the crossed nerves. This revolutionary week changed *Merzenich's* life. He realized that he, and the dominant neuroscience at the time, had fundamentally misinterpreted how the human brain forms maps to represent the body and the world. If the brain map can normalize its structure in response to abnormal information, the prevailing view that we are born with a programmed system must be wrong. The brain had to have, all of it plasticity and consequently neuroplasticity would allow a reprogramming of functions that were previously thought unalterable. More than that, neuroscience has brought to the field a new model of human development, where changing the paradigm of reality of the individual with a reprogramming could alter the entire chemistry of the body's organization systems and, with this, the whole body could regenerate with programmed and focused commands for healing.

The Power of the Word, the Quantum Claims of Healing that we have studied in various therapeutic tools, especially in integrative therapy, can no longer be looked upon with disdain by conventional science, because it itself proves them.

The Quantum of Words

According to the Oxford *Languages data, the* definition of Archetype is the original transcendent model or specimen, which functions as the essence and explanatory principle for all objects of material reality. From the therapeutic point of view, we use the strength of common-sense concepts to strengthen the programming for a desired effect, but we must pay attention to the reality of the subject who presents himself as a patient.

The whole structure of the programming that we are going to introduce you in the fields of information must respect, in a first approach, your belief system, so that there can be acceptance and openness to treatment. As we have already seen, it is possible to use harmful concepts and transmute into something that can be harnessed, if it is in the right quantities. This requires an attentive and creative therapist, but it becomes an easy process for the practitioner with practice. After opening to programming, we have an infinite field of therapeutic possibilities to use, always looking slowly at the patient's needs. I will leave in this book a physical, mental, emotional, and spiritual approach to this programming. For this we will use knowledge at the level of physical anatomy, neuropsychology, energetic anatomy and the strength of the archetype in the word.

We, as human beings, possess immense power in our words, which we often underestimate. When we express ourselves in a positive way, our subconscious is able to turn those words into concrete actions and accomplishments. And it is precisely this dynamic that can be understood by quantum physics, which shows us how words have a force and vibration of their own, capable of influencing our reality.

By utilizing positive words in our communication, we are activating our positive thoughts and creating an energetic vibration that attracts good things like happiness, prosperity, and love into our lives. It is an immense power and at the same time so simple, that it can make a great difference in our life.

Quantum physics teaches us that everything is energy, and that everything in the universe has a vibration of its own. And the words we use have an energetic vibration, which can be both positive and negative. This vibration of words can influence our environment and even our health. Everything in the universe is connected by a network of energetic vibrations, and it is precisely our personal energy that can affect this network. When we speak positive words, we are increasing our own energy, and consequently, influencing the energy around us.

Positive affirmations are a way to use words as a tool to create a more positive and abundant reality. Affirmations can be used in many areas of our lives, from health to money to love and happiness.

When we make a positive affirmation, we are programming our subconscious to believe in this reality, which makes it much easier to manifest these desires. It's as if we create a mental map to achieve our goals, and our subconscious acts as a guide on that journey.

The words we use not only influence our thoughts and emotions but can also directly affect our physical health. Science has already proven that words have a direct impact on our immune system and even on the expression of our genes.

When we use negative words, we are creating an energetic vibration that can affect the health of our body. On the other hand, positive words and affirmations can help us strengthen our immune system and promote healing.

Now that we understand the strength and vibrancy of words, we can begin to utilize them as a powerful tool to transform our lives. For this, it is important to become aware of our thoughts and words, and always choose those that have a higher vibration.

Input Programming

When we are starting the therapeutic process, we must pay attention to the patient's receptivity to the therapy and although this is closely linked to a good anamnesis, it also involves opening the field to a good reception of information in all physical and energetic systems. Confidence with projection of good results in healing, translated theologically as faith, is of paramount importance as well. If you use it on yourself, you must understand a whole scientific context that has been brought here in the book and that leaves no doubt regarding the efficiency of the programming of the fields of information, which when well assimilated as a reference is fully accepted by our metaphysical anatomy. On the other hand, if you are a therapist, in addition to a good anamnesis, you should pay attention to empathy towards the patient and the patient towards you. A good therapeutic relationship, where trust and energetic entanglement are present, are halfway for the consultant to surrender to his healing.

The human body is made up of simple structures like cells, even the most complex ones like the systems of organization that make up the organism. Namely, the level of organization of the human body is as follows:

cells, tissues, organs, systems and organism. Each of these structures consists of a hierarchical level up to the formation of the whole organism and are important to note for the therapeutic process of quantum statements. In the CQM® Method we have the habit of starting our physical healing programming at the cellular level, since they are the basis of the whole structure. Opening the field to cellular receptivity is an excellent start to facilitating healing.

Field Deprogramming

When it is necessary to "delete" information from the reference plan, we always have a long way to go. It is not because it is difficult to cancel beliefs and patterns of behavior, but rather because we often act in the field of what is not conscious. And realize that "erasing" does not mean that the individual will lose a certain bad memory, or that he will miraculously cease to have certain behavior harmful to him. That's not it. To erase is to resignify. Stop impacting harmfully.

When a certain concept ceases to make sense to us, we naturally stop using it and this is what happens with deprogramming. A reframing of concepts, beliefs, behaviors so that they cease to make sense to the individual, who looks at them in another way, and starts to have different verbalizations, attitudes and behaviors, which in a new reality now make more sense.

When I use the regressive technique in therapy, according to the concept of *the CQM® Method,* this is what I do and it does not matter therapeutically if the consultant lived a hundred, five hundred or a thousand years ago a certain experience. It is important to perceive the cause of certain harmful behavior and "erase" it from the individual's system, reframing and changing its reality.

When we talk about Healing, we cannot forget the metaphysics of the systems of organization of the human body, because whether the state is unhealthy physical, mental, emotional or spiritual, it will always leave a record in the *somatizing* body. This factor is so important that we decided at the CQM® Institute to create a specific course to study the physical body with all its metaphysical processes. And this study is not just about looking at the *somatizing* picture and dropping a concept related to its characteristics. The analysis has to be much deeper. An unhealthy state, as we have already seen, is not only based on the symptoms and characteristics of the place where it settles. Until it happens, many *psybiocosmic transformations* take place in the individual's information fields. And they even go through changes in *somatizing* tissues not directly linked to the clinical picture and internal issues that are often disregarded in the diagnostic process. And that's why I bring here the system-by-system programming, which despite being still something very superficial, already brings a component of very deep therapeutic application.

Physical Systems

Bone System, our base, structure, organization

The Bone System is the basis of our third dimensional structure. Without it we would not have the immense possibilities to interact on our planet, for physical reasons, nor to achieve many of the goals we set ourselves. This observation alone gives us an understanding of the metaphysical functionality of this system.

But the Bone System has a much deeper metaphysical function. When a new being is formed, after the cell multiplication of the zygote, the phenomenon of formation of the embryonic leaflets occurs. Embryonic leaflets or germ leaflets (ectoderm, endoderm, and mesoderm) are layers of cells that give rise to the organs and tissues of living beings and that arise in the embryo stage, more precisely during gastrulation, between the third and eighth weeks of gestation in the case of humans. Already here begins the process of somatization of the physical body, through the information captured by the surrounding morphic fields, both of the environment in which the embryo is inserted, as well as the relationships it has, both with parents and the relationships of the parents with other individuals and will be reflected in the formation of bones, muscles, brain and skin, to then spread through the remaining tissues until complete formation of the embryo into fetus. From this comes the importance of studying during the anamnesis the gestation phase of the patient, because it brings a deep richness to the diagnosis.

Muscular System, the action and manifestation

When we analyze the metaphysics of a system, an organ, or an anomaly function (treated as an unhealthy state) we have to look deeply into its physical function to see how it is influenced psychosomatically. In the case of muscles, they are what give us movement and allow us to manifest all the processes of interaction with the environment. It is also they who make the so-called automatic or involuntary movements of the body. So, we can affirm that its metaphysical function is one of action and manifestation. The area where the anomaly is installed, confers its property, for example, if it is in the foot, are issues of action and manifestation in what serves us as a basis, of support, which goes through familiar beliefs and patterns, for example, but also of general organization. If it's at arm level, it's about work issues, in the hand of detail and talent and so on. We have noticed and compiled dozens of cases in which people who have difficulty dealing with things that are beneficial to them, by self-sabotage, have chewing problems at the level of the muscles, especially in the masseter, which is responsible for the movement of the jaw. This clearly shows us the difficulty in processing the information and letting itself be nourished by it and this is because the masseter has this function in the physical body, of maceration of the food bolus so that the nutrient is later removed in the process of digestion. So in this case, the involvement of quantum affirmation is in action and manifestation.

Cardiac System, emotional processing

Traditionally, the study of the communication pathways between the head and the heart has been approached from a rather one-sided perspective, with scientists focusing primarily on the heart's responses to the brain's commands. We learn, however, that the communication between the heart and the brain is actually a dynamic, continuous, bidirectional dialogue, with each organ continuously influencing the function of the other and these the remaining *somatizer*, where a third brain, the gut, enters.

Research from the HeartMath Institute, based today in Boulder Creek, California, has shown that the heart communicates with the brain in four main ways: neurologically (through the transmission of nerve impulses), biochemically (through hormones and neurotransmitters), biophysically (through pressure waves), and energetically (through electromagnetic field interactions). Communication along all of these channels significantly affects brain activity. In addition, research shows that the messages the heart sends to the brain can also affect physical, mental and emotional performance.

In the view of physiologist and researcher Walter Bradford Cannon, when we are excited, the mobilizing part of the sympathetic nervous system energizes us to fight or flee, which is indicated by an increase in heart rate and, in quieter moments, the calming part of the parasympathetic nervous system calms us down and slows the heart rate. Cannon believed that the autonomic nervous system and all related physiological responses moved according to the brain's response to any stimulus or challenge. Presumably, all of our internal systems are activated together when we're excited and we calm down together when we're at rest and the brain is in control of the whole process. Cannon also introduced the concept of homeostasis. Since then, the study of physiology has been based on the principle that all cells, tissues, and organs strive to maintain a static or constant steady-state condition. However, with the introduction of signal processing technologies that can acquire continuous data over time from physiological processes such as heart rate (HR), blood pressure (BP), and nerve activity, it has become apparent that biological processes vary in complex, nonlinear systems. ways, even during so-called steady-state conditions. These observations have led to the understanding that optimal and healthy function is the result of continuous, dynamic, and bidirectional interactions between multiple neural, hormonal, and mechanical control systems at the local and central levels. Taken together, these dynamic and interconnected physiological and psychological regulatory systems are never truly at rest and are certainly never static. If the brain is the processor that works the cognitive process and gives us the references of reality, the heart is the processor of the feelings that are produced through the experiences that shape our individual reality.

Digestive System, interrelational reflex

In Traditional Chinese Medicine, digestion processes are viewed differently from the way we think about them in Western medicine. According to this ancient system of medicine, the food consumed is initially processed by the meridian of the stomach organ, where it is "ripened" or broken down into its useful (treated as "pure") and residual (treated as "impure") components.

Of these, the useful parts are directed to the organ-meridian system of the spleen, where they are transformed into nutrients, energy (Qi), blood and fluids that the body needs. Meanwhile, waste products are directed to the small intestine and finally to the large intestine for excretion.

In the final part of the digestive process, the meridian system of the small intestine organ continues the decomposition of the food that has been started in the stomach and directs any useful matter to the spleen for transformation and distribution, and the waste to the large intestine for excretion through the feces. So here we have one of the processes of relationship with the outside, in the form of food, that is, of the most direct interaction. The way we interact with our reality, how we embrace, how we work, how we root and nourish ourselves from the interrelationship impacts directly with our digestive system. If we connect metaphysical knowledge with the chakra that is associated with it, the solar, we easily realize that this system is a social headquarters, as if it were our living room. We talk so often that it's hard to digest an idea, or that we're chewing on the situation to solve it and we've never stopped to understand what it means, have we?

Respiratory System, the acceptance or rejection of the external source

Your lungs are the pair of pinkish-gray spongy organs in your chest. When you inhale, air enters the lungs and oxygen from that air moves into the blood. At the same time, carbon dioxide, a waste gas, moves from the blood to the lungs and is exhaled (exhaled). This process, called gas exchange, is essential to life and demonstrates the first function of functional respiration. Inhale what is beneficial to us and breathe out what is harmful to us.

The lungs are the centerpiece of your respiratory system. Your respiratory system also includes the windpipe, chest wall and diaphragm muscles, blood vessels, and other tissues. All these parts make breathing and gas exchange possible. Your respiratory system is a network of organs and tissues that allow the exchange of oxygen with the outside, feeding this "fuel" to the cells through the blood. The most common anomalies include allergies, diseases by viruses and bacteria or infections and if we go to do the metaphysical reading all of them represent a resistance of the individual to his reality and this is always presented by a difficulty in processing the feelings. That is why it is very common for sadness, discouragement, anger to settle in the lungs and degenerate into complicated clinical pictures.

Nervous System, the highway of information

The nervous system represents a network of communications of the organism, all of them interconnected and electrical, because information passes from synapse to synapse through an electrical phenomenon.

It is formed by a set of organs of the human body that have the function of capturing the messages, called receptors, capturing stimuli from the environment, interpreting, and archiving the experience in what we call the acquisition of knowledge or cognitive process. Consequently, he elaborates answers, which can be given in the form of movements, sensations, or observations.

The Nervous System is divided into two fundamental parts: central nervous system and peripheral nervous system. The central nervous system (CNS) is responsible for receiving and processing information. It consists of the brain and spinal cord, which are protected by the skull and spine, respectively. The peripheral nervous system (PNS) is one of the divisions of the central nervous system. Its function is to capture and transmit information from this to other organs and to specific parts of the body. The function is carried out through the nerves and nerve ganglia. So the way we interpret reality is binding for the "archiving" of information in the *somatizing* body, that is, both the CNS and PNS will capture and transport the message and transmit it according to what are their personal beliefs. This intricate electrical system that we all possess is, in fact, an embodiment of the subtler energetic channels that are part of the anatomy invisible to the common eye.

Endocrine System, the transmitter of personal reality

The Endocrine System is the set of glands responsible to produce hormones that are released into the blood and travel through the body until they reach the organs on which they act. In synergy and cooperation with the nervous system, the endocrine system coordinates all the functions of our body. The hypothalamus, formed by a group of nerve cells located at the base of the brain, makes the integration between these two systems.

The endocrine glands are in different parts of the body: pituitary, thyroid and parathyroid, thymus, adrenals, pancreas and the sex glands, so they intersect with other systems of organization. We can understand then that when a hormone-producing organ does not do its job, there is a blockage at any level, according to the characteristics of the hormone or neurotransmitter.

Working on our Health Metaphysics course, we pored over each of the hormones and neurotransmitters and came to some pretty interesting conclusions. Let us put here some of them, to explain their metaphysical function.

Dopamine is a neurotransmitter in the catecholamine and phenylethylamine family that plays several important roles in the brain and body. The brain contains several dopaminergic pathways and one of them plays an important role in the behavioral system that is generated in the pursuit of reward. It is involved in the control of movements, learning, mood, emotions, cognition and memory and is therefore a regulator of the meaning that is given to reality. Dopamine dysregulation is related to neuropsychiatric disorders such as Parkinson's disease, in which there is scarcity in the nigrostriatal dopaminergic pathway, and in schizophrenia, in which there is excess dopamine in the dopaminergic pathway in the mesolimbic and scarcity in the mesocortical pathway, that is, dopamine deficiency begins in the lack of motivation, for not feeling rewarded or able to acquire learning, just as its excess is provoked by states of drunkenness of power, by arrogance or austerity and emotional frigidity (which is released in large quantities in order to balance the system).

Oxytocin is a hormone produced by the hypothalamus and stored in the posterior pituitary, and has the function of promoting uterine muscle contractions during childbirth and the ejection of milk during breastfeeding, but it is released by men and women in actions that promote feelings of love, social union and well-being and has also become known as the love hormone, for these characteristics. Their lack is closely linked to feminine energy, lack of emotional and creative processing and isolation, while their excess leads to feelings of possession, obsession with something or someone or the extreme and unregulated need for fun and social contact.

Serotonin is a biological molecule of the neurotransmitter monoamine group synthesized in the serotonergic neurons of the central nervous system (CNS) and enterochromaffin cells. It is also found in various mushrooms and plants, including fruits and vegetables, and the individual can resort to natural supplements for replacement, if in need.

Serotonin plays an important role in the central nervous system as a neurotransmitter in inhibiting anger, aggression, body temperature, mood, sleep, vomiting, and appetite.

These inhibitions are directly related to the symptoms of depression. Among the main functions of serotonin as a neurotransmitter is the function of regulating appetite through satiety, balancing sexual desire, controlling body temperature, motor activity and perceptual and cognitive functions. Serotonin intervenes in other neurotransmitters known as dopamine and noradrenaline, which, at levels below the reference values, can cause symptoms such as distress, anxiety, fear, aggression, as well as eating problems, which usually appear suddenly and for no apparent reason. Serotonin also beneficially intervenes in bone density parameters. So we can assess that serotonin is a hormone that regulates personal organization and will.

Endorphins are basically a neurohormone produced by the pituitary gland. Being known, popularly, as pleasure hormone, endorphins are largely responsible for triggering sensations of pleasure, good mood, happiness and, consequently, more well-being and quality of life, and everything that can produce this hormone is a complement to a better healthy condition. Although it is generated naturally, some activities, such as the practice of physical exercises can intensify and increase its production. Its main function is to inhibit irritation and stress.

In addition, it also naturally reduces body tension and the feeling of tiredness, helping to combat emotional issues such as anxiety and depression. We can easily conclude that procrastination and laziness are at the basis of the anomaly of the balanced production of this hormone, as well as the lack of activities that provoke us states of satisfaction and gratitude.

Excretory Systems, the great recyclers

Here we will include two systems that work the residual expulsion, that is, the expulsion of harmful substances to our body. In the case of the excretory and urinary systems and although they have other functions, both biological and metaphysical, we will focus on this aspect. The excretory system is formed by the kidneys and urinary tracts and is responsible for eliminating waste that the body sees as not useful, after going through the process of digestion of food. Then, the excretory system eliminates substances that are in excess in the body, seeking a process called "dynamic equilibrium", which is routine and natural in this system of organization. The urinary system is formed by the kidneys and urinary tracts (ureters, urinary bladder, and urethra), and is responsible for the production and elimination of urine, so that it filters the "impurities" from the blood. Both expelling the harmfulness of the body, so in metaphysical terms, if there is any anomaly in these systems, we can say that we are facing an individual who resists expelling what is harmful to him, not only what is ingested as physical food but also what he ingests energetically and that result from his intimate and social experience.

Reproductive System, the prosperity expander

The human reproductive system is divided into the male reproductive system and the female reproductive system, although both have the same function, that is, the reproduction of the species. Thus, the male is formed by the testes, epididymis, vas deferens, seminal vesicles, prostate, urethra and penis; while the female reproductive system is composed of the ovaries, uterus, fallopian tubes and vagina.

Considering its characteristics and functions, connecting to the chakra that influences its functioning, the sexual, we can realize that this system reflects the balance of the masculine and feminine energies in the individual. I always like to remember that balance is made in the immediate experience, in the here and now, that is, in no subject does this balance constantly occur in a ratio of 50/50 (male/female). According to their needs, the ratio of masculine and feminine energy is searching, and even the 10/90 ratio can be of balance because at that moment the individual needs more feeling and creativity than his mental and the manifestation of his intentions. This balance makes the subject have more focus and more clarity at all levels, which facilitates good decision-making that is essential for their prosperity processes at all levels.

Lymphatic and Immune System, the dividers of the Self and the We

When I present here these two systems as dividers of the Self and the We, I speak of personal protection and empowerment. When we are empowered, both physically and energetically, we do not to anything that invades our personal bubble and this is because of the time we maintain our vibration (vibration is the time that we can maintain a certain frequency, without breaks). Both systems depend on us looking at ourselves as sacred, as temples, as gods so that they function well and thus protect the physical body.

The immune system is composed of a set of elements of the human body that work together to defend it from bacteria, viruses, microbes, and diseases that only impact our body if they find fertile ground to progress, which often happens when we intimately tender acids, projecting this acidity into the *somatizer*. This system is then a barrier against foreign bodies, the shield of the human body.

The lymphatic system is a complex network of vessels that carries lymph through the body and in conjunction with the immune system, the lymphatic system helps protect immune cells. In addition, it is responsible for the absorption of fatty acids and the balance of fluids in the tissues, which allow, for example, their regeneration. When in anomaly the system enters into an inflammatory process of the lymphatic vessels that are known as lymphangitis and that can have multiple causes, infectious or not. The failure of the distribution of lymph by the body appears in large numbers in individuals who do not honor their roots, their ancestors, in short, their genealogy.

Integumentary System, the revealer of the way I look at myself

The integumentary system, where the largest human organ resides, the skin, helps regulate the temperature of the human body and is responsible for the sensitivity and perception of the third dimension (along with the nervous system) but above all protects the body, creating a barrier to external aggressions and preventing the loss of fluids. It is the element of impact between the outside and the inside of the being and this speaks volumes of its metaphysical function. The way it impacts what we receive from the outside, how it is recorded, whether it hurts on any level, is linked in all systems and is reflected in our skin. It is almost always metaphysically linked to problems of self-confidence, self-esteem, overcharging, feelings of non-belonging, and lack of competence at various levels. A regular example of this type of anomaly is when the body is overexcited at puberty with the amount of doubt that is placed in the formation of the persona of the individual. Yes, the issue is hormonal, but it is also an imbalance, which begins in the mental and emotional bodies. Another interesting point of view from the metaphysical point of view is the fact that the hairs "squat" when we are in protective movements and lift when we are in deep states of reception, which comes with another physical manifestation, the goosebump.

Emotional Systems

Never, as in the present day, has psychosomatic disorder been so present as a cause of non-health states. This disorder is a psychological condition that involves the occurrence of physical symptoms, usually without medical explanation, of a biochemical nature, but which has begun to be observed as originating in emotional states pushed to the limit. People with this condition may have excessive thoughts, feelings, or worries about the symptoms — which affects their ability to function well. Psychosomatics believe that their problems are caused by medical conditions. They tend to visit health care providers frequently for tests and treatments, often without receiving a diagnosis, which can lead to frustration and distress.

Several studies point out that certain things can make people more likely to have somatic symptoms, such as chaotic lifestyle, difficulty recognizing and expressing emotions, childhood neglect, history of sexual abuse, substance abuse (such as alcoholism or drug addiction), among others. And it was due to the high number of cases worldwide of people with psychosomatic disorder that we began to study the influence of emotions on healthy and unhealthy states. A new window was opened here in research at the level of integral health and it was realized that although closely linked, the emotional and mental bodies are not impacted in the same proportion always. That is, both interact in the referencing of the stimulus, but they do not always enter an unhealthy state by this impact.

Emotions are important for human survival. It is argued that most patients will have an emotional response to their illness, but anxiety and depression are unlikely to represent the experience of most patients, as they seem to want to make believe. We have about 450 emotions cataloged as impacting our routine and that reflect the anomalies of our subtle bodies, especially the mental, emotional and physical. It is curious that most studies focus on two important negative emotions, fear and sadness, and perhaps this is why their psychopathological associates, anxiety and depression, are associated. Problems diagnosing anxiety and depression in practice are highlighted. It is claimed that the emotional reaction to the disease is normal and that the emotions expressed probably contain clues to individual adaptation. It is argued that, around health, emotions should be evaluated as healthy reactions to a threat to survival and deserve to be studied from this perspective, if we want to better understand the reaction and adaptation to the patient's individual disease.

"I think, therefore I am" is perhaps the most repeated and well-known phrase in Western philosophy.

According to an article in *Scientific American*, the French polymath, Descartes, and other dualistic philosophers proposed that although the mind controls our physical interactions with the world, there is a clear boundary between body and mind; our physical form is only the temporary residence of our immaterial soul. But centuries of science have argued against body protectors. Body and mind seem inseparable. The findings of a new study by a Canadian team published in the journal *Cancer* suggest that our mental state has measurable effects on our bodies — and more specifically, on our DNA.

The researcher leading the research, *Linda E. Carlson*, Ph.D., and her colleagues found that among breast cancer patients, participation in support groups and focused *mindfulness* meditation so that practitioners focused on current thoughts and actions without judgment, ignoring past and future concerns is related to telomere length retention. Telomeres are the stretches of DNA that cover our chromosomes and help prevent them from degenerating — biology teachers often compare them to the plastic tips of shoelaces. The short telomeres themselves are not known to cause specific diseases, but they shorten with age and are shorter in people with cancer, diabetes, heart disease and high levels of stress. Given this, what we want most is for our telomeres to be intact.

In *Carlson*'s study, breast cancer survivors who were distressed were divided into three groups. The first group was randomly assigned to an 8-week cancer recovery program consisting of meditation and yoga; the second to 12 weeks of group therapy in which they shared difficult emotions and promoted social support; and the third, which was the control group, receiving only a 6-hour stress management course. A total of 88 women completed the study and had their blood analyzed for telomere length before and after the interventions. Telomeres were maintained in all treatment groups but shortened in the control groups. Previous work has suggested this association. A study led by diet and lifestyle guru *Dr. Dean Ornish* from 2008 reported that the combination of a vegan diet, stress management, aerobic exercise, and participation in a support group for 3 months resulted in increased telomerase activity in men with prostate cancer, telomerase being the enzyme that maintains telomeres by adding DNA to the ends of our chromosomes. More recent work on meditation has reported similar findings. And although small and not randomized, a 2013 follow-up study by Ornish, again looking at prostate cancer patients, found that lifestyle interventions are associated with longer telomeres. The biological benefits of meditation go far beyond telomere preservation. Carlson's previous work has found that in cancer patients, mindfulness is associated with healthier levels of the stress hormone cortisol and a decrease in compounds that promote inflammation. In addition, as she points out, "there are healthier people in a *work-based* mindfulness stress reduction program shown to produce higher antibody titers to the flu vaccine than controls, and there has been promising work looking at the effects of *mindfulness* on *AIDS* and diabetes." Previous findings also show that high stress increases the risk of viral infections — including the common cold — as well as depression and cardiovascular disease. The therapeutic potential of the mind-body intersection is well known. Biofeedback — in which patients with sensors learn to have emotional awareness and control over various physiological functions — has been around for decades and is used to treat pain, headache, high blood pressure and sleep problems, among several other conditions. And, of course, there's the placebo effect, the complicated but very real psychobiological benefit achieved from the expectations of a patient's treatment, rather than the treatment itself. While optimistic that meditative and social approaches are emotional means for better physical well-being, and not just psychological, *Carlson* is quite assertive. "The significance of maintaining telomere length in this study is unknown. However, I think processing difficult emotions is important for emotional and physical health, and this can be done both through group support with emotional expression and through the practice of mindfulness meditation," she says. *Carlson* wonders if telomeric changes with mental roots are long-lasting, if the same patterns would be true in other cancers and conditions, and what the effects of mental intervention would be if offered at the time of diagnosis and treatment — all questions she hopes to answer pursuit.

We have here then that the way we mean and reference our emotions directly impacts our physical health.

Recent studies in humans and animals suggest that epigenetic mechanisms mediate the impact of the environment also on the development of mental disorders associated with emotions. Therefore, we hypothesize that polymorphisms in epigenetic regulatory genes affect stress-induced emotional changes. All of this underpins David Hawkins' model *of the Map of Consciousness, commonly called the* Hawkins Scale of *Emotions,* which you probably already know and which he brought up in his book *Power vs Force8.* In the first three chapters, Dr. *Hawkins* presents the background, science, and major components of the Consciousness Map. Two of the key concepts you'll find are field of attraction and field of dominance. Each person is born with a calibrable level of consciousness, which is an energy field within the infinite field of consciousness. In fact, everything in the universe constantly emits an energy pattern of a specific frequency that remains forever, and we now have a means to calibrate energy fields as to their relative strength, similar to what is done with a photometer.

The technique Hawkins uses for the calibration of consciousness is the living clinical science of muscle testing, which utilizes the human nervous system and the life energy expressed through the acupuncture energy system as the necessary sensitive biological measuring instrument. Simply put, in the presence of truth, the musculature of the body becomes "strong." In contrast, it becomes "weak" when confronted with falsehood (which is the absence of truth, not its opposite). This is a quick answer that quickly reveals the degree of veracity of anything. Integrity of intent is required to conduct the test accurately. The Consciousness Map is a reference guide to the spectrum of consciousness, mapping calibrated energy levels, similar to how a thermometer measures heat levels, a barometer measures atmospheric pressure levels, and an altimeter measures elevation level. Measurements are not based on opinion or relativistic perception. Because they are stationary, they form an absolute scale.

Anything can be calibrated and placed somewhere along the scale as a number. An important statement about the infinite field of consciousness is that it represents the Absolute against which everything else can be calibrated by degrees. Calibrations do not establish the truth; they merely confirm it.

In the Map of Consciousness, each level of consciousness is calibrated on a logarithmic scale of energetic power (in base 10), ranging from 1 to 1,000, where 1 indicates existence and 1,000, at the top of the Map, indicates the highest level that it has ever graced the planet; it is the energy of Jesus Christ, Buddha and Krishna, according to what is studied in terms of the metaphysics of the avatars. The level of Shame (20) is at the bottom, near death, and the level of Courage (200) is the critical point of truth and integrity. Love (500) is the gateway to spiritual realm.

The level of Courage (200) marks the shift from negative to positive energy. It is the energy of integrity, *self-honesty* and true empowerment. The levels of consciousness below Courage are anti-life (strength), while the levels above it supports life (power). We tend to look for people above the critical level of 200. We say they are "high" and appreciate their "positive" energy. Your environment is safe and clean. Animals are attracted to them. They have that aura and positively influence everyone around them. On the level of Courage, the negative feelings have not all disappeared, but there is enough energy to deal with them because the person has regained self-adequacy. The quickest way to move from the bottom up is by aligning yourself with truth and love.

Eighty-five percent of the world's population is calibrated below 200, which explains the vast suffering of the planet. Humanity, fortunately, is saved from self-destruction by the calibrated minority on positive levels counterbalances the weight of negativity. For example, one individual at the level of Love (500) counterbalances 750,000 individuals below 200. The significance of each person's inner evolution, then, becomes obvious, as does the urgency to get out of the sick states below 200.

The great Swiss psychoanalyst C. G. Jung, noting the ubiquity of archetypal patterns and symbols, deduced the "collective unconscious," a bottomless subconscious reservoir of all the shared experiences of the entire human race. We can consider it a vast and hidden database of human consciousness, characterized by powerful universal patterns of organization. The great promise of the database – to explore everything that has ever been experienced anywhere in time – is its ability to "know" just about anything when it is "asked", or to access that information spontaneously when there is a need. This is where we explore emotion as a starting point for calibration in balance and for access to healing. We are all everything and everything belongs to us, if we "melt" ourselves in the constant waves of information that are between us.

Information Field Programming

FIELD OPENING STATEMENTS

Our body is an intricate energy system that intersects, collides and flows in every way, creating the condensation we call matter. This complex quantum tangle creates every nanosecond frequency sequence that can be accessed through a personal resonance code that we can read through dowsing, for example. This code makes access to the healing field more effective, but it is not essential to the therapeutic process. With precise commands we can have almost the same effectiveness to work on the facilitation of healing.

1. I am a curious human being and open to continuous learning.
2. I'm always willing to explore new ideas and perspectives.
3. I choose to expand my awareness and increase my understanding of the world around me.
4. I allow myself to be open to new experiences and adventures.

5.   I am grateful for all the opportunities life presents me with to grow and learn.
6.   I trust my intuition and am open to receiving guidance and wisdom from others.
7.   I believe in my ability to process information critically and make wise and informed decisions.
8.   I choose to keep my mind open and free from prejudices and judgments.
9.   I am a valuable and unique human being, able to contribute in a meaningful way to the world.
10.   I am always looking for ways to grow and improve as a person and I am open to all the possibilities that   life   has   to   offer.

BELIEFS DEPROGRAMMING

1.   I am able to create the life I desire.
2.   I deserve love and happiness in my life.
3.   I am worthy and sufficient just as I am.
4.   I can learn and grow from all the challenges I face.
5.   I trust in my ability to make wise and healthy decisions.
6.   I believe in myself and my potential to achieve my goals.
7.   I allow myself to try new things and expand my comfort zone.
8.   I am grateful for all the positive things in my life and focus on the abundance that surrounds me.

9.   I release all limiting beliefs that prevent me from moving toward my best version.

10.   I trust the universe to guide and support me on my journey of personal growth and fulfillment.

HARMFUL PATTERNS DEPROGRAMMING

1.   I deserve healthy, loving relationships in my life.

2.   I am able to free myself from harmful patterns and create positive habits.

3.   I love and respect myself enough to set healthy boundaries.

4.   I allow myself to be vulnerable and ask for help when needed.

5.   I am responsible for my choices and actions and can change my behavior.

6.   I believe in my ability to overcome challenges and adversity.

7.   I'm grateful for all the lessons I've learned along my journey.

8.   I forgive myself and let go of the guilt and shame of the past.

9.   I choose to cultivate positive, loving thoughts toward myself and others.

10.   I deserve to live a happy and healthy life, and I am committed to making choices that lead me down that   path.

UNHEALTHY STATES DEPROGRAMMING

1. I choose to focus on positivity and gratitude in my life.
2. I am deserving of love, happiness, and well-being.
3. I allow myself to relax and rest when my body and mind need it.
4. I can control my thoughts and emotions to live a healthier life.
5. I focus on solutions and opportunities instead of problems and obstacles.
6. I am grateful for my health and well-being and take steps to maintain them.
7. I choose to surround myself with positive, supportive people who help me grow and thrive.
8. I forgive myself for my mistakes and choose to learn from them instead of feeling guilty.
9. I am a valuable and unique human being, worthy of love and respect.
10. I trust myself and my ability to handle challenging situations and overcome them.

SELF-ESTEEM BLOCKS DEPROGRAMMING

1. I am worthy and deserving of love, respect and happiness.
2. I choose to love and accept myself completely as I am, with all my qualities and imperfections.
3. I am grateful for all the good things in my life and appreciate the amazing person I am.
4. I focus on positive, constructive thoughts that help me feel more confident and secure in myself.
5. I choose to release any limiting beliefs that may be holding back my self-esteem from growing.
6. I am responsible for my own happiness and am committed to making choices that make me feel good about myself.
7. I trust my intuition and am open to receiving praise and recognition from others.
8. I allow myself to express my needs and desires clearly and assertively.
9. I believe in my ability to achieve my goals and dreams regardless of the challenges.
10. I deserve to live a full and happy life, and I am committed to making choices that lead me down this path of self-esteem and self-confidence.

MENTAL BLOCKS DEPROGRAMMING

1. I can overcome any mental obstacle and achieve my goals.
2. I allow myself to be creative and explore new ideas and solutions.

3. I choose to release self-doubt and trust in my abilities and talents.
4. I'm grateful for all the lessons I've learned along my mental journey.
5. I focus on positive, constructive thoughts that help me achieve my goals.
6. I am responsible for my own life and am committed to making wise and informed decisions.
7. I trust my intuition and am open to receiving guidance and wisdom from others.
8. I allow myself to be vulnerable and ask for help when needed.
9. I believe in my ability to overcome mental challenges and adversity.
10. I deserve to live a happy and healthy life, and I am committed to making choices that lead me down this mentally healthy path.

EMOTIONAL BLOCKS DEPROGRAMMING

1. I choose to be brave and face my emotions head on.
2. I allow myself to feel all my emotions without judgment or repression.
3. I am grateful for all the emotional experiences that have helped me grow and learn.

4. I focus on positive thoughts and feelings that help me find inner peace.
5. I choose to release the emotional pain and move on with my life.
6. I am responsible for my own happiness and am committed to taking the actions necessary to achieve it.
7. I trust my intuition and am open to receiving guidance and support from others.
8. I allow myself to be vulnerable and ask for help when needed.
9. I believe in my ability to overcome emotional trauma and find healing.
10. I deserve to live an emotionally healthy life and am committed to making choices that lead me down that path.

SPIRITUAL BLOCKS DEPROGRAMMING

1. I am a unique and valuable soul with a significant purpose in this world.
2. I allow myself to connect with my spirituality and find meaning and purpose in my life.
3. I am grateful for all the spiritual experiences that have helped me grow and learn.
4. I focus on positive thoughts and feelings that help me find inner peace and spiritual balance.

5. I choose to release any limiting beliefs that may be impeding my spiritual growth.
6. I am responsible for my own spiritual journey and am committed to taking the necessary actions to move forward.
7. I trust my intuition and am open to receiving guidance and support from others.
8. I allow myself to explore different spiritual practices and philosophies to find what resonates with me.
9. I believe in my ability to find spiritual peace and happiness regardless of external circumstances.
10. I deserve to live a spiritually fulfilling life and am committed to making choices that lead me down that path.

KARMA DEPROGRAMMING

1. I deserve love, happiness, and abundance in my life.
2. I focus on positive, healthy actions that create good karma.
3. I choose to forgive myself and others to release negative karma.
4. I am grateful for all the opportunities life presents me with to learn and grow.
5. I trust the universe to guide me toward my highest good.

6. I allow myself to live in the present moment and release attachment to the past and the future.

7. I am an evolving spiritual being and I am committed to growing and expanding my consciousness.

8. I choose to surround myself with positive, supportive people who help me create good karma.

9. I am responsible for my choices and actions, and I choose to act according to my highest good.

10. I believe in my ability to turn negative karma into positive through my choices and actions.

Metaphysical Programming of the Organism

CELLULAR PROGRAMMING

1. My cells are strong and resistant, able to fight off any pathogens that might enter my body.
2. My immune system is efficient and effective in protecting my body from disease and infection.
3. My body produces healthy, functional cells to replace old, damaged cells.
4. My nervous system is balanced and able to regulate my bodily functions properly.
5. My body produces optimal levels of hormones and neurotransmitters to maintain my emotional and physical balance.
6. My cardiovascular system is strong and healthy, able to carry nutrients and oxygen to all parts of my body.
7. My respiratory system is efficient and able to provide enough oxygen for my cells to function properly.
8. My digestive system is strong and able to absorb important nutrients from the foods I eat.
9. My muscles and bones are strong and healthy, able to sustain my body and allow me to move with ease.

10. My body can regenerate and heal itself, and I am committed to taking healthy steps to support the positive programming of my cells.

TISSUE PROGRAMMING

1. My tissues are healthy and able to regenerate properly, ensuring rapid healing of wounds and injuries.
2. My muscle tissues are strong and flexible, allowing me to maintain good posture and perform physical activities with ease.
3. My bone tissues are dense and tough, protecting my internal organs and allowing me to move safely.
4. My nerve tissues are functional and capable of transmitting electrical signals quickly, ensuring an efficient nervous system.
5. My blood tissues are healthy and capable of carrying nutrients and oxygen to all parts of my body.
6. My lymphatic tissues are efficient in removing toxins and preventing disease.
7. My connective tissues are strong and able to hold my joints and organs in place.
8. My fat tissues are healthy and able to store energy and regulate my body temperature.
9. My cartilaginous tissues are sturdy and flexible, protecting my joints and allowing me to perform gentle movements.

10. I am committed to maintaining a healthy diet and an active lifestyle by supporting the positive programming of my body tissues.

ORGAN PROGRAMMING

1. My heart is strong and healthy, able to pump blood efficiently to all parts of my body.
2. My lungs are efficient at exchanging oxygen and carbon dioxide, ensuring that my cells receive enough oxygen to function properly.
3. My brain is healthy and able to process information and control my bodily functions properly.
4. My liver is healthy and able to filter and metabolize toxic substances in my body.
5. My kidneys are efficient at filtering waste and regulating the balance of fluids and electrolytes in my body.
6. My thyroid is healthy and able to produce thyroid hormones in adequate amounts, keeping my metabolism in balance.
7. My adrenal glands are healthy and able to produce stress hormones in adequate amounts, regulating my stress response.
8. My pancreas is able to produce insulin and regulate my blood sugar levels appropriately.
9. My stomach is healthy and efficient at digesting food, allowing my body to absorb the nutrients it needs.

10. My skin is healthy and able to protect my body from infections, maintain hydration and regulate body temperature.

Bonus. I am committed to maintaining healthy lifestyle habits by supporting the positive programming of every organ in my body.

SYSTEM PROGRAMMING

1. My nervous system is strong and healthy, able to transmit information quickly throughout my body through electrical and chemical signals.
2. My endocrine system is efficient in producing and regulating hormones, ensuring that all bodily functions are in balance.
3. My cardiovascular system is healthy, ensuring proper blood circulation to deliver nutrients and oxygen to all parts of my body.
4. My respiratory system is efficient at gas exchange, allowing my body to receive oxygen and get rid of carbon dioxide.
5. My digestive system is healthy, allowing for proper absorption of nutrients and elimination of waste.
6. My kidney system is efficient at filtering waste and regulating the fluid and electrolyte balance in my body.
7. My immune system is strong and efficient, able to protect my body against disease and infection.

8.   My musculoskeletal system is healthy and able to provide structural support, mobility, and strength to my body.
9.   My lymphatic system is efficient at removing fluids and waste, helping to maintain the health and immunity of my body.
10. My integumentary system (skin) is healthy and able to protect my body from infections, maintain hydration, and regulate body temperature.
11. My reproductive system is healthy and functional, able to produce gametes (reproductive cells) and ensure fertility through the proper regulation of sex hormones like estrogen, progesterone, and testosterone.

Bonus. I am committed to maintaining healthy lifestyle habits by supporting the positive programming of all of my body's organization systems.

Energy Programming

Chakras – Metaphysical Programming

Root chakra: I can materialize my purpose and organize myself effectively to achieve it.

Sex chakra: I express my creativity freely and maintain a healthy balance between the feminine and masculine energies within me.

Solar chakra: I maintain healthy relationships and am able to realize my true identity and reality.

Heart chakra: I am able to deal with my emotions in a healthy way and connect deeply with the feelings of others.

Laryngeal chakra: I communicate clearly and effectively and am able to listen to and respect the opinions of others.

Frontal chakra: I maintain a clear and objective perspective of reality and am able to make rational decisions with ease.

Crown chakra: I feel connected with my intuition and maintain a transcendental relationship with the universe.

Chakras – Energy Balance

Root Chakra (Muladhara): I am safe and secure, and I trust in my connection to the Earth.

Sex Chakra (Swadhisthana): I am creative and express my sexuality in a healthy and positive way.

Solar Chakra (Manipura): I have self-confidence and self-esteem, and I trust in my personal power.

Heart Chakra (Anahata): I love and I am loved, and I maintain the balance between giving and receiving love.

Laryngeal Chakra (Vishuddha): I communicate my truth with clarity and authenticity and listen with empathy.

Frontal Chakra (Ajna): I trust my intuition and my inner wisdom, and I see life with clarity and perspective.

Crown Chakra (Sahasrara): I am a spiritual being connected with the divine source, and I feel peace and harmony in my being.

Chakras – Hormonal Balance

Root Chakra (Muladhara) - Adrenal Gland: I feel safe and confident in my physical existence, balancing the production of adrenaline and cortisol.

Sex Chakra (Swadhisthana) - Gonadal Glands: I am creative and express my sexuality in a healthy and positive way, balancing the production of estrogen and testosterone.

Solar Chakra (Manipura) - Pancreatic Gland: I have self-confidence and self-esteem, and I trust in my personal power, balancing the production of insulin and glucagon.

Heart Chakra (Anahata) - Thymus: I love and I am loved, and I maintain the balance between giving and receiving love by strengthening the immune system and the production of T lymphocytes.

Laryngeal Chakra (Vishuddha) - Thyroid: I communicate my truth with clarity and authenticity, and listen with empathy, balancing the production of thyroid hormones, which regulate metabolism and energy.

Frontal Chakra (Ajna) - Pineal Gland: I trust my intuition and my inner wisdom, and I see life with clarity and perspective, balancing the production of melatonin, which regulates the circadian rhythm.

Crown Chakra (Sahasrara) - Pituitary Gland: I am a spiritual being connected with the divine source, and I feel peace and harmony in my being, balancing the production of all the hormones that regulate the functioning of the other glands and organs of the body.

Subtle Bodies – Metaphysical Programming

Physical body: I take care of my physical body with love and attention, feeding it with healthy foods and practicing exercises and attitudes that strengthen it.

Etheric body: I keep my etheric body strong and balanced, creating a protective shield of energy around me and moving away from negative environments and people.

Emotional body: I allow myself to feel and process my emotions in a healthy way, without repressing them or running away from them, seeking emotional balance in all situations.

Lower mental body: I feed my mind with positive and constructive information, cultivating creativity and the ability to formulate hypotheses and solutions to the challenges I face.

Higher mental body: I connect my higher mind to the wisdom and intuition of the universe, allowing my consciousness to expand and take me to new heights of understanding and realization.

Akashic Body: I honor and respect my personal history by learning from the lessons of the past and using that wisdom to build a better future for myself and others.

Atmic Body: I trust my intuition and the guidance of my inner master, recognizing that I can fulfill my dreams and live a full and meaningful life.

Subtle Bodies – Alignment with the chakras

Physical body: I keep my physical body in balance, aligning my root chakra to feel safe and rooted, and my crown chakra to connect with divine wisdom.

Etheric body: I strengthen my etheric body by balancing my sex chakra to increase my vitality and creativity, and my solar chakra to protect me from negative energies.

Emotional body: I harmonize my emotional body, opening my heart chakra to love and be loved, and my laryngeal chakra to express myself authentically and truthfully.

Lower mental body: I balance my lower mental body by activating my frontal chakra to have mental clarity and intuition, and my laryngeal chakra to communicate my ideas clearly and assertively.

Higher mental body: I connect my higher mental body, aligning my crown chakra to connect with divine wisdom, and my cosmic portal chakra to connect with my Higher Self and receive spiritual insights and guidance.

Akashic Body: I integrate my akashic body, balancing my laryngeal chakra to clearly communicate my personal story and understand the lessons learned, and my crown chakra to connect with divine wisdom and understand my life purpose.

Atmic Body: I tune into my *atmic* body, activating my crown chakra to connect with my Inner Master and receive divine guidance, and my heart chakra to live in love and compassion for myself and others.

Subtle Bodies – Alignment with Organism Organization Systems

Physical body: I keep my physical body in balance, aligning my skeletal system to maintain the structure and stability of my body, and my nervous system to control and coordinate bodily functions.

Etheric body: I strengthen my etheric body by balancing my circulatory system to ensure an efficient circulation of vital energy in my body, and my immune system to protect me from disease and infection.

Emotional body: I harmonize my emotional body, balancing my limbic system to regulate my emotions and feelings, and my endocrine system to control hormone production and maintain emotional homeostasis.

Lower mental body: I balance my lower mental body by activating my central nervous system to process information and reason clearly and logically, and my limbic system to integrate emotions and thoughts in a balanced way.

Higher mental body: I connect my higher mental body, aligning my autonomic nervous system to connect with divine wisdom and receive spiritual insights and guidance, and my endocrine system to produce hormones of well-being and happiness.

Akashic body: I integrate my akashic body, balancing my peripheral nervous system to understand my personal history and lessons learned, and my endocrine system to produce hormones of gratitude and understanding.

Atmic Body: I tune into my atmic body, activating my sympathetic nervous system to connect with my Inner Master and receive divine guidance, and my limbic system to live in love and compassion for myself and others.

Morphic Fields – Cleaning, Harmonization and Reprogramming

1. I am able to clear and harmonize my morphic fields, bringing balance and well-being to my life.
2. My morphic fields are always in resonance with the positive energy of the universe, attracting positive experiences and people to me.
3. I am grateful for the morphic fields that shape and shape my being, for they are a manifestation of the creative power of the universe.
4. By connecting with nature, I strengthen my connection to the morphic fields that sustain all life on the planet.
5. I rely on the process of morphic resonance that connects me with the previous forms of my species, allowing me to constantly learn and evolve.

6. By meditating and visualizing my cleansed and harmonized morphic fields, I reprogram my mind to attract more love, peace, and happiness.
7. I believe I can positively influence the morphic fields around me, helping to create a more harmonious and balanced world.
8. By taking care of my body and mind, I also take care of my morphic fields, ensuring that they are always vibrating at a high frequency.
9. I am part of a global network of interconnected morphic fields, and so my positive actions affect the world around me.
10. I honor the collective memory of my species and seek to learn from the previous forms, so that I can contribute to the evolution and harmony of the planet.

Akashic Field – Cleaning and Reprogramming

1. I am able to clear my mind of old memories and limiting beliefs.
2. My mind is becoming clearer and more harmonized every day.
3. I allow my energies to be balanced and aligned with the Universe.
4. I am open to receiving the messages from my higher self and letting go of what no longer serves.
5. I release the past and focus on the present and future with positivity.

6.   I am connecting with my true essence and freeing myself from negative patterns.

7.   My soul is healing and expanding every moment.

8.   I am grateful for the lessons I have learned from my past experiences.

9.   I am willing to forgive and let go of all the people and situations that have wronged me.

10.   I am able to reprogram my mind and replace old patterns with positive, constructive thoughts.

11.   I am able to access the information of my past lives and release all that no longer serves.

12.   I am willing to heal the wounds of the past to live fully in the present.

13.   My mind is open to receiving positive and healthy information from my past lives.

14.   I am able to grasp the lessons of my past lives and use them to grow and evolve.

15.   I am releasing all the negative emotions and beliefs I carry from my past lives.

16.   My soul is freeing itself from all the limitations I have acquired in my past lives.

17.   I am able to transmute the negative energies of the past into light and love.

18.   I am becoming more and more aware of my past lives and the information they contain.

19.   I am willing to face and release all the negative emotions and patterns of my past lives.

20.   I am grateful for the opportunities my past lives have given me to grow and evolve as a human being.

21. I am grateful for the valuable information I receive from my akashic field and use it to grow and evolve.
22. My mind is open and receptive to the positive energies of the akashic field.
23. I can access my akashic field to heal my emotional and physical wounds.
24. I am freeing myself from limiting patterns and beliefs that prevent me from reaching my full potential.
25. My soul is expanding and becoming more and more connected to the akashic field.
26. I can manifest the life I desire through connection with my akashic field.
27. I rely on the process of cleansing, harmonizing, and reprogramming that takes place through my akashic field.
28. I am becoming more aware of my past lives and the lessons I can learn from them.
29. I am open and willing to work in collaboration with my akashic field to achieve harmony and inner balance.
30. I am grateful for the akashic field and all the possibilities it offers for my personal evolution and growth.

Forgiveness

To the other:
1. I forgive you for any pain you may have caused me in the past.

2.   I choose to release any resentment I may have against you and move on.

3.   I recognize that you are also human and that you can sometimes make mistakes, just like me.

4.   I choose to focus on the love and compassion I have for you rather than any anger or resentment.

5.   I completely forgive you and hope we can continue to have a healthy and positive relationship.

To locations:

1.   I choose to forgive this place for any painful memory I may have associated with it.

2.   I release any negative energy that may be connected to this location and choose to focus on the present.

3.   I honor this place and all the experiences I've had here, but I choose to let go of anything that binds me to the past.

4.   I choose to allow positive energy to flow in this place and hope to create new happy memories here.

5.   I thank this place for all the lessons I have learned here and choose to move forward without carrying any weight from the past.

To events:

1.   I choose to forgive any difficult situation I have faced in the past and release any resentment or hurt associated with it.

2.	I recognize that we all go through difficult times in life and choose to focus on the learning and growth that these situations have brought me.
3.	I choose to release any guilt or shame that may be associated with past events and allow myself to move forward lightly.
4.	I choose to live in the present and let go of any worry or anxiety that may be linked to past events that I cannot change.
5.	I thank all the situations and events in my life, both good and bad, as they have helped me become the strong and resilient person I am today.

Reprogramming the Family System

1.	I choose to forgive my family for any pain they may have caused me in the past and move forward with love and compassion.
2.	I recognize that my family is imperfect, as am I, and I choose to focus on the positive things instead of the negative.
3.	I honor my family's roots and the stories that brought us here, and I choose to move forward with gratitude rather than resentment.
4.	I choose to connect with my family in a healthy and authentic way, creating stronger and lasting bonds.

5.   I recognize that we are all different and that this can lead to conflict, but I choose to embrace our differences and find common ground.

6.   I choose to let go of any expectations I may have of my family and accept them for what they are.

7.   I choose to be honest and transparent with my family and hope they can also be honest with me.

8.   I choose to create an environment of love and respect within my family so that we can grow and thrive together.

9.   I choose to communicate my needs and boundaries in a clear and respectful way so we can have a healthier relationship.

10.   I believe in the power of reconciliation and choose to work to heal any wounds of the past and create a happier and more harmonious future with my family.

Ancestry

1.   I am willing to let go of the limiting beliefs of my ancestors.

2.   I release the negative patterns of my ancestors and open myself up to new possibilities.

3.   I can heal the wounds of my ancestors and create a better future for myself and my family.

4.   I choose to live my life based on my own beliefs and values, rather than blindly following family standards.

5.   I am grateful for the valuable teachings of my ancestors, but I am willing to leave behind what no longer serves me.
6.   I recognize that the negative patterns of my ancestors are not my fault, and I am willing to let them go.
7.   I am strong enough to face any negative pattern that may be present in my family and overcome it.
8.   I deserve to live a full and happy life, free from the limiting beliefs of my ancestors.
9.   I believe I can create my own destiny and am not limited by my family's past.
10.   I am willing to strive to change my limiting patterns and beliefs to create a better future for myself and future generations.

Prosperity

Physical Health

1.   I am healthy and strong in every aspect of my being.
2.   I feed myself nutritious and healthy foods that support my physical well-being.
3.   My body is a sacred temple and deserves care and respect.
4.   I exercise regularly and keep my body in good shape.
5.   My immune system is strong and healthy, and it protects me from disease and infection.

6.   I sleep well every night, which is essential for my physical and mental health.

7.   I can find the right balance between work and rest to keep my body healthy.

8.   I take proactive steps to prevent illness and injury by getting regular check-ups and maintaining a healthy lifestyle.

9.   I believe in my ability to heal my body and overcome any physical health challenges I may face.

10.   My body is a powerful instrument to allow me to fulfill my dreams and live the life I desire.

Mental health

1.   I am mentally strong and resilient, able to face any challenges life may bring.

2.   I allow myself to take time to take care of my mental health because I know it is essential to my overall well-being.

3.   I am grateful for the positive things in my life and choose to focus on them.

4.   I accept my imperfections and love myself unconditionally.

5.   I communicate clearly and effectively, which allows me to express my feelings and needs.

6.   I set healthy boundaries for myself and others to protect my mental health.

7.   I practice self-compassion and am kind to myself during difficult times.

8. I seek professional help when needed and am willing to receive support and guidance for my mental health.
9. I take regular breaks to relax and recharge my mind and body.
10. I choose to live in the present and don't allow negative thoughts or worries about the future to affect my peace of mind.

Emotional Health

1. I allow myself to feel all of my emotions, recognizing that they are part of my life journey.
2. I can deal with my feelings in a healthy and productive way.
3. I am open to connecting emotionally with others, which helps me build meaningful and fulfilling relationships.
4. I am grateful for all the emotional experiences I have, including the challenging ones, as they help me grow and evolve.
5. I create an emotionally safe environment for myself and others where vulnerability is valued and respected.
6. I practice self-compassion and forgive myself when I make mistakes or face emotional challenges.
7. I focus on the present and choose to let go of the negative emotions of the past that no longer serve me.

8.   I am aware of my emotional triggers and take steps to protect myself from them or deal with them in a healthy way.
9.   I practice gratitude every day, which helps me cultivate a positive, optimistic outlook.
10. I believe I am able to thrive emotionally, creating a full and fulfilling life for myself.

Finance

1.   I deserve to have a prosperous and abundant financial life.
2.   I believe in my ability to attract and create wealth in my life.
3.   I am grateful for all the financial opportunities that come my way.
4.   I trust the universe to guide me toward an abundant financial life.
5.   I know my worth isn't tied to my money, but I deserve to be paid properly for my work and talent.
6.   I release any limiting beliefs about money and embrace positive thoughts about abundance and financial prosperity.
7.   I take proactive steps to achieve my financial goals and create a financially secure future for myself and my family.
8.   I am grateful for the financial blessings I have already received and maintain a positive attitude toward my financial future.

9.   I am willing to learn more about finances and make informed decisions about my money.

10. I believe in myself and know that I can overcome any financial blockage I may encounter in my path.

General Relationships

1.   I deserve loving and meaningful relationships in my life.

2.   I am grateful for the positive relationships I have in my life and am open to meaningful new connections.

3.   I communicate my needs and feelings clearly and respectfully in my relationships.

4.   I create an emotionally safe and positive environment for myself and others in my relationships.

5.   I strive to understand the perspectives and needs of others in my relationships.

6.   I am willing to resolve conflicts constructively in my relationships.

7.   I value individuality and autonomy in my relationships, allowing people to be who they are and respecting their choices.

8.   I am open to compromises and teamwork in my relationships, to achieve our goals together.

9.   I actively nurture my relationships, devoting time and effort to strengthening them.

10.   I believe I am able to thrive in my relationships by creating meaningful and lasting connections in my life.

Love Relationships

1.   I deserve a healthy and happy loving relationship in my life.
2.   I am grateful for my partner's presence in my life and for all that he or she brings to our relationship.
3.   I communicate my love and affection on a regular and genuine basis to my partner.
4.   I strive to understand and support my partner's needs and dreams.
5.   I am open to compromises and negotiations in our relationship so that we can grow together.
6.   I practice empathy and compassion in our relationship, recognizing the challenges my partner faces and supporting him or her through them.
7.   I respect my partner's individuality and autonomy, allowing them to be who they are and respecting their choices.
8.   I am willing to do my part to keep our relationship healthy and happy by investing time and effort into it.
9.   I believe we can overcome any challenges together, further strengthening our relationship.

10.   I am committed to building a prosperous and loving future with my partner by creating unforgettable memories together.

Abundance

1.   I deserve an abundant and prosperous life in all respects.
2.   I believe that abundance is my divine right, and I am open to receiving it.
3.   I am grateful for all the blessings and abundant opportunities that arise in my life.
4.   I trust the universe to guide me toward an abundant and prosperous life.
5.   I focus on positive thoughts of abundance and reject thoughts of scarcity and limitation.
6.   I am always open to learning and growing, to attracting even more abundance into my life.
7.   I believe in myself and my abilities to create an abundant and prosperous life.
8.   I maintain a positive attitude toward money and wealth, recognizing that money is a tool to create more abundance in my life and in the lives of others.
9.   I recognize and celebrate the abundant things in my life every day, cultivating a mindset of gratitude and appreciation.

10.   I am willing to follow my heart and pursue my dreams, confident that abundance will flow naturally into my life.

New Reality Programming

1.   I can create a new reality in my life, aligned with my deepest goals and dreams.
2.   I trust in the inner wisdom that guides me toward a more authentic and meaningful reality.
3.   I am open to new possibilities and opportunities in my life, ready to create a new reality.
4.   I believe I can overcome any challenges I encounter as I create my new reality.
5.   I am willing to commit and work hard to create a new reality in my life.
6.   I maintain a positive and optimistic attitude, trusting that life always supports me in creating my new reality.
7.   I honor my past and all the experiences that have brought me here, but I am ready to let go of what no longer serves and embrace a new reality.
8.   I am grateful for all the people who support and encourage me as I create my new reality.
9.   I am committed to living my life with authenticity and integrity, aligned with my new reality.

10. I am excited about the infinite possibilities the universe has in store for me as I create my new reality.

Opening Paths and New Possibilities

1. I feel the energy flowing freely through my chakras, opening paths to new possibilities in my life.
2. I am grateful for all the opportunities for learning and growth that arise in my life, allowing me to create new possibilities.
3. I am open and receptive to the positive energies of the universe, which help me create new possibilities in my life.
4. I focus on cleansing and balancing my subtle bodies, allowing new energies and possibilities to flow freely into my life.
5. I honor my connection to the morphic fields by recognizing that my beliefs and thoughts can influence my ability to create new possibilities.
6. I connect with my spiritual and akashic guides, seeking guidance and inspiration to create new possibilities in my life.
7. I am willing to let go of what no longer serves in my life, allowing space for new possibilities to emerge.

8. I trust the universe to guide me toward the opportunities and possibilities that best align with my journey.
9. I maintain a positive and optimistic attitude towards the possibilities in my life, believing that anything is possible.
10. I am grateful for all the blessings and opportunities that the universe presents me, allowing me to create a life full of new possibilities.

I deliver and trust

1. I feel the energy flowing freely through my chakras, opening paths to new possibilities in my life.
2. I am grateful for all the opportunities for learning and growth that arise in my life, allowing me to create new possibilities.
3. I am open and receptive to the positive energies of the universe, which help me create new possibilities in my life.
4. I focus on cleansing and balancing my subtle bodies, allowing new energies and possibilities to flow freely into my life.
5. I honor my connection to the morphic fields by recognizing that my beliefs and thoughts can influence my ability to create new possibilities.

6.   I connect with my spiritual and akashic guides, seeking guidance and inspiration to create new possibilities in my life.
7.   I am willing to let go of what no longer serves in my life, allowing space for new possibilities to emerge.
8.   I trust the universe to guide me toward the opportunities and possibilities that best align with my journey.
9.   I maintain a positive and optimistic attitude towards the possibilities in my life, believing that anything is possible.
10.   I am grateful for all the blessings and opportunities that the universe presents me, allowing me to create a life full of new possibilities.

Using Field Programming

The technique of Positive Affirmations is a tool of great magnitude to transmute limiting beliefs and foster beneficial transformations in both personal and professional life. Nevertheless, it is important to keep in mind that there is no right or required way to employ such a technique.

The therapist or user of this technique can choose which statements to use and in what order, considering individual needs and goals. Some publications recommend a specific order, starting with a field opening and ending with the delivery of intentions, but this is not a must.

It is recommended, however, to always start with a field opening, which consists of an affirmation that helps a person to connect with the universal energy and open himself to new possibilities. For example, one might use the expression, "I am part of the universe and am receptive to receive all the blessings and opportunities it affords me."

As for the statements themselves, it is important that they are formulated in a positive way, in the present and in the first person, as if they were already a reality. Instead of saying, "I'm not afraid to speak in public," it's more effective to say, "I'm an excellent communicator and I feel confident when speaking in public."

Finally, it is recommended to end with the surrender of intentions, which is an affirmation that reinforces the person's commitment to make the desired changes. For example, one might say, "I commit to making the changes necessary to achieve my goals and live the life I desire."

In short, the Positive Affirmations technique can be a valuable tool for fostering positive change in personal and professional life. It is important to remember that there is no right or required way to employ it and that it is important to adapt it to individual needs and goals. The use of a field opening, and the delivery of intentions are recommended, but the rest of the affirmations can be customized according to the situation.

Good use of the tool and that it can be of contribution to your life.

1. Bibliography

1. Emotional intelligence: The revolutionary theory that redefines what it is to be intelligent, Goleman, Daniel, Editora Objetiva, 2012
2. The Biology of Belief, Lipton, Bruce H., Butterfly Publishing, 2007
3. Spontaneous Evolution. Lipton, Bruce H., Butterfly Publishing, 20013
4. The Messages of Water, Emoto, Masaru, Isis Publishing, 2004
5. Scientific American, Cook, Gareth, 2016
6. "The Benefits Associated with Gratitude," Fox, Glenn, University of Southern California
7. Journal of Alternative and Complementary Medicine, 2014
8. Power Vs Force, Hawkins, David R., MD, PhD, Editora Hay House, 2014

Contact the author

e-mail: Frederico.honorio@gmail.com
instagram: @fredericocostahonorio
facebook: /fredericohonorio

Printed in Great Britain
by Amazon

40842446R00076